TESTIMONIALS

Hadad's *The Power of PR Parenting* is for the working mom and dad who want a little less chaos and a little more impact in their everyday life at home. Her lovely chit-chat-before-bed style invites parents to enjoy a personal conversation with the author who applies well-worn business techniques to create a smoother, happier life. None of us gets a parenting manual, but this book offers a fresh perspective that gives well-lived insights that will help us all write fabulous stories as we raise competent and successful kids. A welcome addition to your nightstand.

Kathy Hirsh-Pasek, Ph.D.
Author: *Becoming Brilliant* (APA Books, NYT Best Seller),
& *Making Schools Work* (Teachers College Press).
Professor of Psychology, Temple University &
Senior Fellow, Brookings Institution.

"*The Power of PR Parenting* by Marjie Hadad is read with bated breath, as it leads us through a fascinating personal and family story to a deep understanding of how principles from the field of public relations can be highly relevant when applied to our family life. Thus, this book is unique in its ability to convey in a clear and simple manner how these principles can be wonderfully applied in the work of raising children.

This book is a dialogue between the reader and the author, which I read with pure pleasure. In an exciting, empathetic, and close-to-our-everyday-parenting-experiences way, the author equips parents with the tools to properly manage family crises, even life-threatening ones, to build self-confidence in our children, to prepare our children for the future and to help them develop positive introspection and a world view that is empathetic and compassionate. It also equips parents with tools that will allow them to help their children exercise good judgment in risky situations where they themselves are not present.

I strongly recommend reading the book. I have no doubt that it will give leverage and support to many parents."

—Dr. Dafna Katzir-Goldenboum,
educational psychologist and psychotherapist

"Riveting. Very suspenseful at times and leaves the reader wanting to skip ahead or read faster to see what happens. It is also thought provoking. Marjie is really on to something here very important for working moms. They can absolutely use Marjie's PR expertise to help teach and model for their children, young and grown, skills and strategies that are useful for thriving in life."

—Lorry Leigh Belhumeur, Ph.D.,
licensed psychologist, author, inspirational speaker,
coach, *Mastering Resilience* creator and trainer

"As a national publicist and TV talk show producer, I couldn't put down *The Power of PR Parenting*. It grabbed me right away, which is not easy to do. I loved Marjie's PR gems and the stories that she shares that we all go through as publicists. Her positive outlook even in a bad situation is quite admirable. I'm also the parent of two kids. What a smart idea and how clever to apply these skills to everyday parenting. Brilliant! All folks in

THE POWER OF PR PARENTING

HOW TO RAISE CONFIDENT, RESILIENT, AND SUCCESSFUL CHILDREN USING PUBLIC RELATIONS STRATEGIES

BY

MARJIE HADAD

CHICAGO · NEW YORK · PARIS · ROME

The Power of PR Parenting: How to raise confident, resilient, and successful children using public relations strategies.

Copyright © 2023 by Marjie Hadad

All rights reserved. No part of this publication may be reproduced, distributed, or transmitted in any form or by any means, including photocopying, recording or other electronic or mechanical methods, without the prior written permission of the author, except in the case of brief quotations embodied in reviews and certain other non-commercial uses permitted by copyright law.

Neither the publisher nor the author is engaged in rendering professional advice or services to the reader. The ideas, suggestions and procedures provided in this book are not intended as a substitute for seeking professional guidance. Neither the publisher nor the author shall be held liable or responsible for any loss or damage allegedly arising from any suggestion or information contained in this book.

The information in this book is intended for educational and entertainment purposes only. It is not intended to be a substitute for the legal, medical or psychological advice of a professional. The author and publisher are not offering professional psychology, medical or legal advice.

Additionally, this book is not intended to serve as the basis for any type of decision or action, which remains solely that of the reader. You should seek the services of a competent professional, especially if you need support for your specific situation.

While best efforts have been made in preparing this book, the author and publisher make no warranty, representation or guarantee with respect to the accuracy or completeness of information contained herein.

The author and publisher assume no responsibility for your actions and specifically disclaim responsibility for any liability, loss, risk or physical, psychological, emotional financial or commercial damages personal or otherwise, which are incurred as a consequence, directly or indirectly, of the use and application of the content of this book. In case studies, some names have been changed to protect the privacy of these outstanding individuals. The stories are told as remembered by the author in tandem with online press reports and other online documentation.

Printed in the United States of America
Hardcover ISBN: 978-1-958714-64-5
Paperback ISBN: 978-1-958714-65-2
Ebook ISBN: 978-1-958714-66-9
Library of Congress Control Number: 2022950011

CHICAGO · NEW YORK · PARIS · ROME

Muse Literary
3319 N. Cicero Avenue
Chicago IL 60641-9998

the industry will learn something, feel validated and for sure chuckle. Brava!"

—Cindy Garnick, Garnick Entertainment Media Group and publicist/producer

"As the former owner of a public relations firm and the mother of three, I found Marjie Hadad's perspective on parenting spot on and very unique in its approach. I marveled at how simply applying these particular business skills to parenting resulted in producing resilient, problem-solving, clear-thinking children. With nearly 30 years of parenting behind me, I wish I had found this book sooner! Not just working moms, but all moms would benefit from this practical and easy-to-read parenting guide."

—Marybeth Bisson, President's Advisory Committee Berklee College of Music, owner of Wicked Craft restaurant, philanthropist, and, most importantly, mother.

"Loved every page. So powerful. Moms will be with their highlighters taking notes."

—Justine Zwerling, proud mother of two and Shore Capital (Capital Markets), Head of Middle East

"As a mum of three juggling managing 4 international companies, a healthy relationship with hubby, entertaining family and friends and dedicating time to my kids, the book opened my mind to considering a new perspective in life. No longer should I get home and try to do everything to disconnect with daily lessons in life that I encounter, but rather this book shows how we should all make an extra effort to merge our professional concepts that work in our corporate lives with our family life at home. The lessons that Marjie took home to her family were contemporary, but writing a book about it and revealing to the world that this method actually works is damn ingenious."

—Daliah Sklar

"Marjie has astutely employed her public relations professional skills in her role as a mother of three. With honesty and humor, Marjie, in her book *The Power of PR Parenting,* shares public relations strategies, the dynamics of her multi-cultural family, and how the intersection of the two has benefitted both her children and herself. Marjie's book, straightforward and captivating, is a must read! I only wish that I had a copy of it when I was bringing up my now grown kids but am happy that it is currently available to help the new generation of working moms. As an educator, I found that *The Power of PR Parenting* opened my eyes to a novel way of thinking and of approaching my teaching with the ultimate goal of inspiring my students and instilling within them confidence, resilience, and a love of learning."

—Beth Yakoby, mother of 3 and history teacher, Princeton Day School.

"As a mother and entrepreneur, I am always looking for new ways to help me ideally support my child. Just when we need it most, Marjie Hadad's captivating *The Power of PR Parenting* offers a unique, fascinating world of parenting strategies, practices and tools to help our children navigate this unimaginable world with more confidence, grace and grit."

—Sara Connell, bestselling author of *Bringing in Finn*

"Entertaining from start to finish, Hadad's book offers a unique look at the intersection of public relations and parenting. A great read for anyone who has a child or knows a child!"

—Alexandra Kuisis, bestselling author of the award-winning book, *Truth Matters, Love Wins: A Memoir*

"Marjie shares a goldmine of parental wisdom mined from her incredibly successful career in International Public Relations. She empowers parents to draw on the skills and wisdom from their own careers and talents and walks them through how to simplify and customize what works for their own unique family. Her quick wit combined with her mama bear love guides parents to find the humor and to share love in even the most challenging situations."

—Wendee Villanueva, entrepreneur and proud homeschooling mother of two

"Marjie inspires women to blend their professional and personal worlds to better balance successful careers with being amazing mothers. Through her gift of storytelling, Marjie shares her unique perspective of using her professional public relations expertise to help her raise her now grown and accomplished children. As a military spouse and mom, Marjie's insight helped me to celebrate all the balls I was juggling while raising my own family. After reading *The Power of PR Parenting*, you will have more ideas how to tackle the expected and the unexpected and to do so with grace and humor."

—Shari Biery, national board-certified health and wellness coach at Alive With Purpose Health & Life Coaching, LLC

"Whether you are a parent, aunt, uncle, cousin, or friend of the family, there is something in here for everyone. Marjie Hadad's The Power of PR Parenting offers relatable and refreshing golden nuggets on how to care for your family, tribe and community. Witty and lighthearted, it burns through tough topics with wisdom and insight."

—Jaymie Velasquez, aunt, godmother, author/engineer

"Through the pages of Marjie's work, the messages of how to parent using the techniques learned in her years of being a public relations expert are clearly presented. From creating written contracts with your children to having candid conversations with them about their safety, Marjie provides working examples and lessons to follow so that a parent's message is understandable and concise. Marjie writes from her own experiences and professional expertise with the intention to help parents bridge and foster life's lessons into effective communication. As a mother of six through a blended family, I feel an especially wonderful part of the writing is the emphasis and reminder for parents to be role models for their children through their own reactions to life's ups and downs."

—Donna Kendrick, author of
A Guide to Widowhood: Navigating the First Three Years

DEDICATION

This book is dedicated to my fellow working mothers, in and out of the house, doing their best to strike a healthy balance between work and parenthood.

This book is also dedicated to my husband, my children and the public relations profession, the combination of which made this work possible.

TABLE OF CONTENTS

Foreword xv

Introduction. xix

Chapter 1: Crisis Management 1

Chapter 2: Rites of Passage: Transactions, Translation
               & Kiddo Copywriting. 21

Chapter 3: Public Speaking & Presentation. 37

Chapter 4: Maintaining Grace. 57

Chapter 5: Keeping Your Cool 75

Chapter 6: Safety and Transparency. 95

Chapter 7: Building Self-Reliance 117

Chapter 8: Showing Up. 135

Chapter 9: Deadlines and Self-Care. 151

Chapter 10: Being Part of the Solution 171

Postscript 185

Acknowledgements. 189

Endnotes 193

About the Author. 195

> "Keep your eye upon the donut,
> and not upon the hole…."

—An Irish proverb first shared with me by my Aunt Nancy Neff when I needed it most. May it guide you as it has me.

FOREWORD

Why should you read this book?

Dear readers, moms, dads, and everything in between,

I have talked to many parents and what links most, if not all of them, is the question—am I doing this right?

I know that sometimes you wonder if you're a good parent, if you could be better, and what you should be doing differently.

Personally, I believe that these questions are confirmation enough that you are a great parent because it means that you care enough to ask them and want to be the best version of yourself for your child. However, we could all use some guidance on how we could better ourselves.

And now you're wondering why you should read this book. Well, let me tell you a little bit about my mom, Marjie.

My mom is kind, caring, confident, and smart. She is a full-time working mom who has given my siblings and me everything we needed and so much more. My mother taught me self-love, confidence, and kindness. She taught me how to communicate with others, speak in public, and function in stressful situations. She allowed me to grow and gave me every opportunity to better myself. She made me feel like there is nothing I can't do or accomplish if I set my mind to it.

But most importantly, she always made me feel loved.

When I faced stressful situations, I would hear her voice and advice and it would enable me to calm down and evaluate the situation and what needed to be done. Hopefully, one day I'll be able to do the same for my children.

There is no handbook to perfect parenting, but I truly believe that this book will soothe some of your worries and will allow you to implement new methods and perspectives that will benefit your life and your children's lives.

And to my mommy—I am so incredibly lucky to be your daughter and I am so proud of you and this book.

—**Noa Lee**

* * *

Have you ever taken a moment to reflect upon your childhood? Looking back, a countless number of factors woven together came to influence the person that you are today. Your environment at school could be an example, the interactions you had with strangers could be another, and for many of us, the presence, or lack thereof, of a parent's love and guidance spelled the prologue for our life's story.

If you are reading this, it is likely that you have already given thought to the way you would like to raise your children. And whether you're expecting a newborn or have several young teenagers keeping your house lively, or somewhere in between, it is only natural that you would want to raise your children to the best of your abilities so that they can reach their full potential.

I would like to share with you why I believe you should read this book and what benefits you could expect to gain by applying the lessons it contains.

Growing up, like most people, I had my ups and downs. Whether academically, socially, or in other myriads of life, things seemed to change constantly. In the midst of all of these changes, there was one thing I knew would always remain the same—an unfaltering constant I've carried with me to this day—the support, love, and lessons I received from my mother.

She taught me to never give up, to speak up if I believed something was wrong, and to follow my dreams no matter what others think. She taught me to celebrate my wins, and more importantly, learn from my mistakes. She taught me kindness, forgiveness, and unconditional love. These and more are lessons I cherish deeply, and in this book, you can find the methods in which to impart them to your children.

I wish you the best and hope you can find lessons that resonate with you and disciplines to pass forward to your young ones.

And to my mom, thanks for everything.

Our children are reflections of the tools we give them with their own light shaping the image we see. Use this book as your toolbox and guide your children to success.

—**Guy Hadad**

INTRODUCTION

One fine spring afternoon, my then 11-year-old daughter was walking to the small market in our suburban neighborhood about a block up the road. On her way, she reached for a piece of fruit from one of the trees that lined the empty street, but it was too high for her to grasp.

As she was on her tippy toes and stretching to reach the prize, a tall man, apparently watching from nearby, walked up behind her, plucked the fruit and handed it to my daughter.

"Thank you," she said to the stranger.

He replied, "You are welcome. I have some candy that will taste better than this in my car. It's just over there." He then tried to further engage my daughter in conversation with hopes that she would follow him.

"No thank you. I'm on my way to the store," she replied and continued quickly on her way, with an eye on the stranger. She didn't want him to know where she lived, so she waited until he had disappeared out of sight and then made a U-turn straight back home to safety.

I was alarmed when she told me what had happened. It was creepy. VERY creepy. Who is this guy? What does he look like? Alert the neighbors! Call the police!

I also exhaled that my girl had kept her cool, put distance between herself and the stranger and, at the first opportunity, ran like the wind to safety. Potential crisis averted.

Exhale, but only halfway. When you are raising kids, there's always something—something to worry about, something to fix, something to teach, something to plan for, something to help with. And each time, we ask ourselves, "How on earth should we handle this?"

How should we handle this? We will ask ourselves this very question regularly throughout our lives because parenthood is a never-ending job where we all have tenure.

I was born, raised, and educated in the United States and started my career in 1986 as a TV journalist. Just under a decade later, I moved from Boston to Jerusalem in January 1995 to begin a new job and an adventure that continues until today.

Prior to my move to Israel, I had been working as the media liaison (public relations representative) at the Consulate General of Israel in Boston and was finishing my master's degree in International Relations at Boston University. In the summer of 1994, I was invited to work in the Policy Planning Department of the Israel Ministry of Foreign Affairs in Jerusalem. My job would include writing background papers for the Oslo Accords bi-lateral talks and speeches for Foreign Ministry dignitaries.

When I was offered the opportunity, I thought: *I'll get paid to do what I just did to earn my master's degree, and it will be for something real and meaningful. Cool!*

In January 1995, I collected my diploma and jumped on an airplane to begin my adventure. This led to meeting my husband Isaac, getting married, and birthing and raising my three multicultural, dual-citizen, Israeli and American kids, Guy, Noa Lee and Maya.

Following my time at the Foreign Ministry, I returned to international public relations and advanced my career through many twists and turns along the way, first at a boutique agency, then later at a very large one, and finally on my own as a consultant.

I have now been a PR pro for 30 years and a working mom for 25. I'm still happily married to Isaac, the kids are now grown and our family dog, Rocky, a tiny, fluffy white Maltese, still pees on the floor on occasion to mark his territory.

When I look at my children today, I see the people they have become, I observe the choices they make, and I watch as they navigate each challenge. In these same moments, I also see the babies, toddlers, little kids, and teens they used to be. I remember the old days and enjoy watching the mega-fast-forward simultaneously.

It was during one of these moments that it hit me: *Throughout the years, I'd applied the practices from my job as an international public relations expert to raise my kids, and they had adopted these same practices to pursue their chosen paths. It wasn't a conscious decision on my part, but wow, it worked and to their advantage.*

But let's back up a moment.

In the early days, I'd consult with other working moms and compare notes to see if the same movie was playing out at their homes and how it was being handled. I found I was not alone, trying to figure it all out.

Do you ever ask yourself, How do I:

- deal with this medical crisis?
- instill self-love and confidence in my children?
- shield my children from harm on and offline?
- prepare my children to be the best people they can be?
- teach my children certain necessary skills that will serve them throughout a lifetime?

- teach my children kindness, goodwill, and grace under fire?
- do all this and remain standing at the end of the day?

I know I asked myself these same questions, and some of them I still do.

Those early days, though, are now ancient history for me, and I'd like you to benefit from my hindsight and experience.

The chapters that follow will show you how public relations practices can provide another way to look at and do things, and maybe serve as a blueprint of sorts to help you find more success and perhaps a little more peace of mind.

Though psychology does find its way into the public relations profession as it does others, I am neither a psychologist nor claim to be one. I am also not a parenting expert, nor do I claim to be one. I am a PR pro who has raised three capable and kind kids. My intention is to offer new ideas and approaches that have worked for me and that I hope will benefit not only your children throughout life but also you, personally and professionally.

We'll have a look at some big-picture issues, which I know can be overwhelming. We'll also talk about those little things that always seem to hit the wrong chord.

We'll go step-by-step and show you, very specifically, how to use PR practices to help solve different types of problems, handle a situation and inspire self-love, confidence and resilience in your child. Stories will be shared, not in chronological order, but as they are relevant to each major topic addressed. We'll also practice together with exercises that you can use at home or wherever you are.

Please don't freak out about the word *exercises*. I promise you, I'm NOT looking to create extra work for you, quite the opposite. Plus, it will be fun! And we are certain to giggle along the way.

I invite you to use what you can now and file what is pertinent for later.

If you don't know anything about PR, then a whole new world is about to open up to you. If you have experience in PR, media, marketing or sales, then you'll learn new ways to apply your existing skills. You might find common denominators between public relations and your own profession that you can use creatively to achieve your goals. And, as you are reading, you might discover superpowers you didn't know you had.

Let's be clear, I am NOT saying I was or am the perfect mom—far from it. And I have made loads of mistakes; in fact, I'm still making them, though hopefully only new ones. Live and learn. We'll talk about all of this too, and the lessons learned, to help you avoid the same pitfalls.

Now back to my epiphany. How do I know that using PR practices has helped my kids? There are many examples, such as how they:

- calmly handle crises.
- strategically open doors and create opportunities for themselves academically, professionally and socially.
- confidently present themselves in all types of forums.
- respectfully and amiably interact with different types of people, of all ages.
- enjoy a process (win or lose).
- methodically and thoughtfully plan for an upcoming event, initiative, or goal, from daily homework to a party to a job interview.

This book will show you how you can teach your kids these exact skills and hopefully experience the same success.

One of my favorite byproducts of their growing up in a PR household, however, is their work ethic and their resulting military service achievements.

My son, Guy, won the "Award of Excellence" at the end of his basic training in the Israel Defense Forces (IDF). He went on to command a special unit. He rose to the occasion multiple times and was always the choice of his unit to present during a visit to his base by someone high ranking.

My daughter, Noa Lee, won the "Award of Excellence" several times during her tour and was nominated for the prestigious "President's Award" for distinguished service in the IDF. I should also mention that her hour-long interview for this award took place just after a major family health crisis. Regardless, she walked into the room of officers sitting behind a long desk, head held high, calm, and pleasantly surprised the panel by greeting each with a handshake and a smile.

My youngest, Maya, received an "Award of Excellence" at the end of 10th grade for community service. Rather than the 30 hours required that year for sophomores, she logged a collective 64 hours between tutoring first graders and telephone calls with their parents, folding clothes at a consignment store as well as handing out flyers and answering questions from angry people, impatient from waiting too long in their cars at the neighborhood COVID drive-through test center.

Yes, they are great kids. Perfect? No. Who is? We're all human and have our strengths and weaknesses. Our house is no different than any other in this respect. And though the window dressing may be different, we all share many of the same core and universal challenges of working parenthood. The difference is how we deal with it all.

Remember the story about my daughter at the top of this introduction? That was Noa Lee. Her reaction to the stranger offering candy in his car was not by chance or random. It was because of one of the many PR practices exercised at home, which we'll visit in Chapter 6: Safety & Transparency. So be sure to read on.

We're all in this together my friend, and by sharing my personal story—the good and the bad (approved for disclosure by my husband and kids)—as well as the finer points of my profession, I am hoping to help make your journey that much easier.

Easier sounds good. Yes? Great!

Please make yourself a coffee, a tea or whatever your choice of beverage, and I'll do the same.

Have a seat, and let's chat!

CHAPTER 1

CRISIS MANAGEMENT

In this chapter:
- Managing crises
- Delegating and relying on your home team
- Remaining calm and in control
- Talking yourself through

It was just after 7:30 a.m. on a Saturday. I was in my usual half coma/half-conscious state at that hour. You see, I am more of a night owl, wide awake at 1 a.m. and dead to the world by 7 a.m. I was nestled in my very comfortable, king-sized bed, which takes up most of the space in our compact bedroom located on the third floor of our townhouse.

The bedroom was glowing with that special kind of drowsy morning dark, where there is just enough light piercing the slightly opened window blind to see everything in the room.

A few minutes earlier, I had been listening to Isaac, my handsome *Sabra* (native Israeli) husband of 23 years at the time, and the love of my life, as he was preparing to go to the gym.

I knew Isaac was *the one* the first time he took my hand as we sat watching a movie at the cinema, just after we had started dating in the spring of 1995. It was like the last scene in *Sleepless *in Seattle* when Tom Hanks first takes Meg Ryan's hand at the top of the Empire State Building. Close up on the hands, then on their eyes, each entranced with the other. Electricity. Magic. I have the same feeling today whenever we hold hands. I wish this for you too.

My husband stands at 6 feet and has the kindest, brightest, orthodontics-free, straight-toothed smile. He's also the nicest guy I know, with many talents. He's an engineer for a tech company by day and an amateur gourmet chef by night. He does the *real* cooking at our home.

(I always say to our guests when comparing our cooking skills, "You'll *eat* with me, but you'll *dine* with him.")

Isaac is a morning person. At the time, he was also significantly overweight, at more than 100 kilos or slightly more than 220 pounds. When I first met him, he was thin. Then came the continuous weight gain from each of our three pregnancies, which HE never dropped. I'm certain this is the same scenario in many households. Yours too? Beware.

Isaac had accepted an invitation from our friend and neighbor to join him at the gym that morning. He was returning from a steamy shower to unkink a pain in his right calf and was starting to get dressed, when he approached his side of our bed, the one closest to the entrance of our bedroom.

"I feel dizzy," he said.

I have vertigo, serious vertigo. So, his declaration didn't raise any red flags for me. Everyone's different though, and it should have.

"If you are dizzy, maybe lie down for a few minutes and skip the gym," I whispered with as much energy as I could, opening my eyes for a split second before closing them again.

Isaac slipped into bed for perhaps a minute or so before I *felt* him get up. He continued getting ready in the little more than arms-length space between the bottom of our bed and our shared light brown, French oak closet that stretched the width of the room.

Then, BOOM!!!

My first thought: *What on earth did that man break in this room that would sound like that?* I quickly scanned my memory. No idea. I sat straight up, now fully awake, my eyes open wide. Isaac was not in sight. Maybe he went back to the bathroom?

"Are you okay?"

No answer.

I got up on my side of the bed to see what was going on. Isaac was lying on the floor in front of our bed, half on his side, half on his back, his head facing the closet.

My public relations crisis management experience instinctively kicked in.

I didn't feel anxious or a surge of adrenalin. I was mostly concerned and puzzled as I tried to understand and process the crashing noise from seconds earlier, along with the deafening silence that followed.

I quickly walked over to Isaac and knelt down to assess the situation. There was a big gash in the center of his forehead, in the shape of a Harry Potter scar, and a pool of blood on the floor in front of his face. His eyes were slightly opened and dazed. I called out his name.

"I can't feel my legs," he whispered.

Clearly, I had an unexpected and enormous emergency on my hands. What to do?

PR Crisis Management Philosophy

In any crisis, we have two choices: freak out or stay calm and take care of business.

In public relations, there are almost daily crises, some bigger and some smaller. And though most aren't life-or-death situations, they can feel like they are. The pressure is immense, with your boss, clients, and colleagues all counting on you to put whatever fire out.

As the PR representative, you are on the front line and need to be strategic, calm, and methodical—or at least appear that way on the outside. Beyond all that, when push comes to shove, it's on you to produce a positive end result.

If we freak out, we risk not only upsetting those around us and delaying damage control but also the agency losing a client or maybe even our own job.

On the inside, your nerves might be fried. But like the old antiperspirant commercial goes, "Never let them see you sweat."

My first PR job, as the media liaison at the Consulate General of Israel in Boston back in the early 90s, provided a wonderful crash course in crisis management. Let's say it the way it is: Israel is always on the hot seat for one thing or another, fair or unfair. I don't want to get into politics or debate the issues, but the reality is, someone or some entity is always there to offer a critical opinion or ask a critical question when it comes to Israel. My job, when such calls came in, was to listen and diplomatically set the record straight accordingly with the position of the government in power.

When it came to the big stuff, I was briefed in advance. On one occasion, I was told it was likely that I'd receive an early morning press call at home the next day. And, sure enough, my phone rang before sunrise at 4 a.m. the following morning. The reporter started firing questions immediately after I picked up.

I interrupted him. "First, good morning," I said in a sleepy and raspy, Demi Moore-like morning voice. "I'm with you; just give me a second to turn on the light and open my eyes." The reporter chuckled understandingly, paused, and chilled out. After a little less than a minute, I was ready. The reporter explained what he wanted to know. It was time to wake up and brief the Consul General, who was expecting my call and ready to interview.

The heat is equally high when working in the commercial agency world. The public relations stakes are enormous for clients, be they businesses, governments, or high-profile people, as well as for the agency, which needs to maintain its retainers.

It's often like moving mountains to convince stubborn and egotistical editors or reporters to fix factual errors. It can be equally challenging to explain to angry clients that they can't take back a published but accurately reported quote they don't like or recall a press release that has already been issued over one of the *paid-for* news distribution services, like Business Wire or PR Newswire.

And then, there are the simply bad judgment calls. I saw this when I was working at a PR firm that was simultaneously servicing two clients with conflicting interests. This ultimately blew up when one discovered this via a press release sent out on behalf of the other.

The proverbial shit hit the fan and quickly flowed down. An all-company meeting was called, and the person who had written and issued the press release was publicly humiliated. That person was me. I was in the *doghouse*, but I wasn't fired.

I continued to do my job as usual, and then, in a perfect example of how quickly circumstances can change, about a month later, another all-company meeting was called where I was publicly congratulated for great work for another client. Go figure.

This crisis was a VERY good lesson for me and has influenced how I work until today. Examples: I won't make something public for a client without written approval to do so; I document activity along the way in the event I have to prove something retrospectively; understanding that no good ever comes from humiliating someone, I do my best to always treat colleagues with respect and kindness; and I turn any mistake into a learning experience.

After this experience, I internalized the pressure from each crisis, less and less each time, until the point where, when crisis reared its ugly face, I would become instantly quiet and calm like still water and go straight to thinking how to problem solve.

I ask myself: How can I fix it? And if I can't fix it myself, I think, who can I get who has the skills to fix it? This is how I handle most situations at work today and as much as possible at home too.

Crisis after crisis after crisis, after enough of these, it's just another crisis, and you just deal with it. And, yes, it can be learned. I wasn't calm about anything growing up. I'd scream and cry when faced with any negative situation, big or small. My mother would always say, "Next time, *act* rather than *react*." I heard it enough times over the years that it finally sunk in. Mom's other crisis-related advice: Ask yourself, how will this affect your life in five years? If it will, then make your pros and cons list and problem solve. If not, then it's not the big deal you think it is, and maybe just let it go.

Applying PR Crisis Management Skills To Parenting

So why is this important, and how do we apply these public relations crisis management skills to parenting?

It's important because if we present a calm demeanor to those around us AND stay calm on the inside too, at least as much as possible, we have the best chance of achieving a positive resolution to a bad situation.

How to stay calm? Just like I talk my clients through difficult situations, I do the same for myself as needed. I have a lightning-quick, private conversation with myself. I encourage myself to stay calm and focused. Then I take a deep breath—maybe a few deep breaths—and onward.

These conversations, which can be out loud or in your head, will likely get quicker and quicker over time, until you can skip them altogether and just instantly launch into crisis mode. Or, depending on the crisis, you may find it helpful to talk yourself through the entire event. Whatever you choose, it's way better than freaking out.

If we freak out, we waste valuable time that could make the difference between life and death. If we freak out, we potentially stress those around us as well as cause them to freak out too, especially our kids.

Has your child ever fallen? And the second after they do, do they look up at you to see your reaction? They are looking for you to tell them if all is okay or not. If you look alarmed, they'll be alarmed. The opposite is also true. If you stay calm, the odds increase that they'll stay calm.

Ask yourself, what scenario do you want to create? Wouldn't you rather have your kid smile, knowing that all is well, assuming that it really is, and pick themselves up and continue playing? And if all is not okay, isn't it better to show them you are confidently in control (even if you are not) to keep your child calm so you can focus on the problem solving?

I remember when my son, Guy, then four years old, slipped on a wet floor in the kids' bathroom, hit his head on the toilet bowl, and split open his right eyebrow. The floor was wet because, not too much earlier, I had given his baby sister, Noa Lee, a bath, and I hadn't completely dried the floor at the end.

My husband raced to the entrance of our bedroom, across from the kids' bathroom in our apartment at the time, screaming my name, clearly angry and afraid. Our poor little boy, now bleeding down his face, stood there too, overwhelmingly alarmed and crying.

I emerged from my own shower, wrapped in a towel, trying to remember what I could about head wounds, which wasn't much. I had grown up with three younger siblings, and we all had had our share of medical dramas back in the day. This, for the most part, was the knowledge I had to go on.

I thought to myself: *Do what you do at work—stay calm. If you are calm, the kid will be calm. Just like when Guy falls, show him with your body language, facial expression, and a confident tone in your voice, that everything will be okay, and this will help to calm him down. If you freak, he'll freak, Isaac will freak even more and then we can spend the next hour fighting, as our son continues to bleed from his head. OY.*

"Are you okay, Guy?" I asked, trying to maintain a normal voice.

He looked up at me and replied, "Mommy, I hurt myself."

Okay, check, check, check. He was alert and verbal and could see me (hopefully, no concussion). So far, so good.

I put a clean dressing on top of his wound, quickly dressed, and drove Guy to emergency, where they finally stitched his wound an hour after our arrival.

During the car ride over, I apologized to Guy for not drying the floor properly. That was on me, and Isaac and Guy were right to be cross.

Look, raising kids comes with all sorts of scrapes, breaks, and bruises, and sometimes even worse. We all have these stories, and probably many of them, be they on the playground, at the swimming pool, on a family trip—the location isn't important. Bottom line, our babies, no matter their age, take their cues from us, and again, we have a choice: freak out or be calm and take care of business.

Public Relations Skill: Remaining Calm While Taking Care Of Business

Remaining calm and taking care of business were exactly what was needed that terrible Saturday morning when Isaac collapsed, bled on the floor, and couldn't move.

I thought to myself, *Well, I can't pick you up.*

And then I asked myself, *Who can I get to help?*

"I am going to call the ambulance," I declared out loud. As I stood up, I listened for my husband to protest. Dead silence.

It was 7:35 a.m. when I called for an ambulance.

My call with emergency lasted exactly three minutes. I shared the details with the lady on the phone in an urgent but steady voice. She instructed me to get a towel, wet it, and press it to my husband's forehead to stop any bleeding. I did as I was told with the first towel I spotted in the bathroom hanging on the towel rack. It was large, white, fluffy, and 100% cotton. After I finished patting Isaac's gash with the wet part, I tried to clean the blood on the marble floor with the dry part. It was a knee-jerk reaction to clean the floor, and I didn't do a very good job. It's weird what you notice or don't notice in times of crisis. I mean, who cares that there's blood on the floor when your husband can't move and is about to take an ambulance ride to the hospital?

When the bleeding had stopped, I began to prepare for the emergency responders, who would arrive at around 7:45 a.m.

PR Crisis Management Practice: Choose Your Team Thoughtfully (Who was home to help and crisis management-ready?)

I was still in my pjs and needed to throw on some day clothes before the paramedics arrived. Someone also needed to answer the door and let them in. But I didn't want to leave my husband in our room alone. Who else could open the door?

I wasn't sure if Guy was at home. By then, he had recently completed his mandatory military service for the Israel Defense Forces and was a university student living with us. He had been out with his friends the night before.

I was sure, however, that my daughter, Noa Lee, then in the middle of *her* mandatory military service, was indeed at home. The night before, she, Isaac, and I had attended a lovely Friday night dinner at the home of the parents of one of her fellow soldiers.

Noa Lee was no stranger to medical or terrorist emergencies by the time her father collapsed. She had started to bleed in the middle of the night at the tail end of the 10-day danger period following a tonsillectomy when she was 15. Without pause or freak out, I rushed her to the hospital where she was treated and discharged by late morning. Noa Lee told me later that this was the crisis management example that solidified her crisis management approach.

Fast forward and it's now the summer before Noa Lee's senior year in high school. In my day, a group of friends would go to the seashore *after* graduation for a week to celebrate. Well, because the kids in Israel generally go to the army within a matter of months after high school ends, they celebrate graduation a year earlier. And rather than a domestic trip to the beach, they traditionally fly to a location abroad for a week of fun. Lucky them!

Noa Lee and her friends chose a pre-planned, pre-paid, beach town party week in Spain. During a day trip to Barcelona on August 17, 2017, they were enjoying morning coffee at a café on the famous La Rambla Street. Next stop: La Sagrada Familia, the famous Gaudí church which should be on everyone's bucket list, no matter their religion. The architecture is simply spectacular.

All were ready to go, except for one in the group, who was still drinking her coffee and insisted everyone wait for her to finish. AMEN that she did. This delay of two minutes or so likely saved their lives.

Standing by the glass window facing the La Rambla promenade, the girls saw the white van the ISIS terrorist had used seconds earlier to mow down locals and tourists in its path, killing 13 and injuring 130. The danger of the situation didn't fully register with Noa Lee and her friends until swarms of screaming, frantic people flooded into the café through the front glass door. Noa Lee and her friends ran from the glass window to the kitchen in the back to take cover. One of her friends tripped along the way and cut her leg, which Noa Lee cleaned and wrapped for her with a bandage that one of the nice café employees had given her. She also tried to calm a young woman with a child, who sat crying next to her.

There were too many people in the coffee shop from a safety perspective, so someone with authority escorted Noa Lee, her friends, and others, through a back passage that led to a hotel not too far away. The girls stayed there until they were instructed by the leaders of their trip to walk to the bus a short distance away that would return them to their beach town. If they didn't show up, they were on their own to find a way back. Meanwhile, the hotel was telling everyone to stay put. Noa Lee and I consulted and together decided she should return to the bus.

Noa Lee and I were in constant contact, by chance, just before the attack, throughout the aftermath, and then for the duration of her walk from the hotel lobby to the trip bus. The situation was out of my control. All I could do was talk her through, help to make any necessary immediate decisions, and hope that the crisis management skills taught at home had sunk in.

To her credit, she remained calm throughout the ordeal and tried to help whomever needed help along the way. So, yes, calm and being of service are skills that you can teach to your kids too.

PR Crisis Management Practice:
Delegate To Your Team & Accept All Help

Noa Lee had had a front-row seat to many of the crises I had to manage, both at work and at home. And, when these involved her, she followed the lead that was provided, well, at least some of the time. Noa Lee tends to dance to the beat of her own drum, if you know what I mean. Sometimes it takes a while to teach these skills, and it certainly doesn't happen overnight. But have faith in yourself and in your kids, that when the moment arrives, like when Isaac collapsed, that they will step up.

So, when I needed help knowing that the medics were on their way for Isaac, I confidently called Noa Lee. She answered her mobile phone with a soft, sleepy voice, "Hello."

"Noa Lee, your father has collapsed. The ambulance will be here in a minute. Please open the door for the paramedics and show them where to go," I requested with a serious, but steady voice.

Rather than the usual reporter inquiry: *What happened? Why? How?* She understood from my tone that there was an emergency and simply replied, this time in a stronger voice, "Okay."

Two paramedics walked through my bedroom door just as I was finishing throwing on the same jeans and shirt I had worn the night before to the dinner party. One was a blonde-haired, short, and stocky woman dressed in uniform. She knelt over my husband's face and asked him if he were diabetic. No. Not diabetic. This lady's questions are the first memories Isaac has after he collapsed. He doesn't remember telling me that he couldn't feel his legs.

With my husband now in the hands of the medical professionals, it was time to prepare him for what clearly would be a hospital stay—who knew how long? Noa Lee appeared at the entrance to my bedroom.

"What else can I do, Mom?" she asked.

"Please find a bag I can put Daddy's things in," I replied. And off she went.

I collected a pair of Isaac's sweatpants, flip-flops, and socks. I also grabbed one of his shirts, a sweatshirt, a toothbrush, toothpaste, soap, and a little towel. My mind was now racing. What else would he need? That's right. His laptop, mobile phone, health group card, and Israeli ID—all downstairs in his work knapsack.

As I was gathering the contents of his hospital bag, Isaac mentioned again that he couldn't feel his legs. I slid my right pointer fingernail the long way down his left foot, from top to bottom. He barely felt it. At least he felt it, though.

It took four very strong people to carry my husband down two full flights of stairs, out the door and up the entrance stairs to the street where the ambulance was parked in front of our house.

Noa Lee was waiting for me at the bottom of the stairs on the first floor.

"Here is the bag, Mom," Noa Lee said, ready for the next assignment.

"Please put Daddy's things into the bag," I requested. She did.

I grabbed Isaac's work knapsack, then the overnight bag from Noa Lee, ran to the ambulance, took my invited spot in the front passenger seat, and we were off to the hospital. We arrived, I think, just after 8 a.m.

Up until this time, I stayed very much in the moment. You have to understand, outside of a crisis, it's very unusual for me to be 100% in the present. I'm always thinking and daydreaming about the past and the future.

So, you may be asking yourself, if your mind is generally all over the place, like for many of us, how is it possible to stay in the moment, not become emotional and keep your focus on getting a job done? One word: Compartmentalizing.

I focused on what was necessary and put emotion to the side. How? No other reason than BECAUSE I HAD TO. I had no choice, just like I had no choice sometimes at work. And you can do this too. I promise you; you have it in you to rise to any occasion, especially if the stakes are high.

As my Aunt Nancy used to say, "Eye on the donut, not on the hole." Meaning, for this purpose, keep your focus on the task at hand and try not to get distracted.

Repeat this to yourself, whenever you are in a crisis, and know that you DO have the ability and the strength to pull it off. After all, you are a parent who multitasks almost every hour of the day and sometimes night. Tap your inner mama bear and get going!

And that's exactly what I did on the morning that Isaac collapsed. I had no choice but to step up. His life depended on it. Two ambulances later, check-in, a full body CT, and several other tests thereafter, my husband was diagnosed with two large embolisms in his lungs. The embolisms had cut off his oxygen. This is why he had lost consciousness and dropped like a falling log.

What I couldn't figure out was how he had managed the gash in the center of his forehead when there wasn't anything on the floor that morning, let alone anything sharp. I learned a week later from our housekeeper that when Isaac had fallen, he had hit his head on the pointy part of the metal handle of the open sock drawer, the one closest to the floor, before ricocheting to the right, smack onto the marble floor.

"Didn't you see the blood on the handle?" she asked me.

I hadn't noticed.

Luckily, she managed to clean the blood off the floor. No stains. Evidence erased. Visual memory erased.

Isaac had been on his way to a heart attack, and the impact of crashing on his forehead had damaged his spinal cord: whiplash and several dents. It took five days to learn if he would be able to walk. He could. But he had lost feeling that would take another year to nearly fully regain.

My husband was in the hospital for a total of ten days, five in the Cardiac ICU, and the balance in the general cardiac ward. For the first four days, I almost never left his side, mainly sleeping in the chair next to his bed that accordioned when my weight wasn't properly distributed.

Luckily, I had help. In addition to close friends and immediate family, all three of our children stepped up and did their part—willingly, thoughtfully, and calmly. We were a well-coordinated team, like the many I have worked with throughout the decades as a publicist.

If you are in a trying situation at home, remember that you don't have to do everything yourself, any more than you have to at work, even though I'm sure you feel like you are doing EVERYTHING sometimes, no matter where you are. I totally get you.

Everyone has their specialty and their function. This is the case in PR, and I suppose in your profession too. Take control of the situation, rather than let the situation take control of you. Delegate tasks and assign responsibilities to those on your team, just like at the office, only now it's your kids, family, and friends. Manage those things that are in your control and try not to think about the things out of your control.

This is what I try to do as a PR executive and what I tried to do at home as well as on the way to and once at the hospital.

For the first several days, our kids would arrive throughout the day or evening with whatever was needed that we had asked for and extras that they had thought of, sometimes on a revolving door, sometimes together.

On the second day, they brought a cake to mark Maya's, our youngest, 15th birthday. We had planned to celebrate the day before at the fancy Asian restaurant in Tel Aviv that everyone was talking about. Noa Lee took care to cancel our reservation, and instead, we stood singing happy birthday and eating a bit of cake next to Isaac in his ICU bed, all wired up to one medical device or another. Our sweet, beautiful birthday girl was a good sport about it, accepting an IOU for a proper celebration in the future, as she, along with the rest of us, prayed for her daddy to recover.

Unprompted, Noa Lee arranged a short-term leave from the military to help with whatever was needed. She relieved me for my first night to sleep at home since "the event" and slept in the "accordion chair" next to her father.

Again, unprompted, our son, Guy, time managed his schedule to attend classes during the day AND take a few overnight shifts at the hospital. By that time, Isaac was in the general cardiac ward, where there was a comparatively comfortable couch for us to crash on.

Through his shift, Guy would half sleep and half listen for anything his father might need.

"Dad, I'm here for you," Guy reminded his father repeatedly.

As for Maya, her job was to stay positive, refrain from any teenage drama, and do as she was told—the *first* time. She did.

In fact, all three sourced the education learned from the various personal and work-related crises we had experienced together during their childhood to maintain calm and focus, do what they could, ask others for help with what they couldn't, and keep a constant eye on the important end goal. The PR crisis management lessons that began when they were babies were being practiced right in front of my eyes. **IT ALL CAME DOWN TO THIS MOMENT.**

Proud mama? Of course. More importantly, it allowed me to breathe, knowing I could count on my *in-home* team.

Thanks to our children, we made it through those ten days. The teamwork was so good that I was able to remain available to my clients for anything truly important. In public relations, the show must go on, crisis or not. I took a client call in the ICU and a Zoom team call in the general ward, medical device beeps in the background when my laptop microphone was not on mute.

Just like when Guy slipped and split his eyebrow on the toilet bowl, when Noa Lee tasted blood following her tonsillectomy, and when Noa Lee had her untimely visit to Barcelona, I did my best during Isaac's "event" to continue providing the best example I could of how one should "act" rather than "react" in a crisis.

PR Crisis Management Takeaways

Let's review: compartmentalize by separating emotion from the event in order to remain calm, assess the situation, set a course of action, stay focused as you do your part, delegate to others as necessary, and where possible, be ready to roll with whatever the job requires. If you need to, talk yourself through it, out loud or in your head, to help you remain calm.

If someone around you is freaking out, depending, either gently assign them a task that is useful to the situation and to keep their mind busy or tell them directly to knock it off or leave.

You can decompress in private along the way, and after all is in order. I burst into tears for a few minutes multiple times to relieve the volcanic-like pressure building inside of me when Isaac was in trouble. Acknowledging the possibilities connected to the situation was overwhelming. I permitted myself the luxury of letting go mainly when I was alone, though a couple of times, the tears started streaming without warning during calls with a certain family member and a close family friend.

Cry, scream, punch a pillow, go out for a walk, enjoy a smoothie with a friend—whatever works for you, as long as it's healthy and legal. Go for it! You have to take care of you too! Otherwise, how can you take care of your family?

Ten days following Isaac's hospital admission, he finally returned home to begin a long recovery, but with a happy ending. As of this writing, Isaac is nearly 100% back to himself and back to work. He's also 15 kilos lighter and maintaining. Not the way I would wish for or recommend to anyone to lose weight, but there you have it.

Life is messy. Working motherhood is especially messy and full of high drama, and every step of the way, it's like being the master of ceremony of a 10-ring circus, 15 rings on some days. It's not easy, and we don't always succeed. I know I don't. Ask my kids. Sometimes I get it right. Sometimes I don't. It's part of being human. Plus, when our babies arrive, they don't come with instructions, and each has their very own special personality and disposition. What works for one doesn't necessarily work for another. It's all one big confusing and wonderful challenge.

Thinking back to their father's "event" and how all three of my kids had stepped up, I knew I had at least done something right. They had learned and applied the PR crisis management lessons well. I was proud of the people they had become, including, as the song "All of Me" by John Legend goes, *their perfect imperfections.*

Believe in yourself. Believe in your kids.

Remember:

- Compartmentalize your emotions and any fear to deal with AFTER the crisis is over
- Focus ONLY on the problem solving, set a course of action and implement without hesitation

- Talk yourself through when needed
- Demonstrate confidence so that your kids know that someone is calling the shots, even if you do not feel in control
- When your kids are in a crisis, help them to assess the situation and choose a course of action, even if you are far away
- Ask for help and accept it as needed
- Eye ALWAYS on the donut—not on the hole

If you would like to practice applying the public relations strategies above to your own story, please use your cell phone camera to scan the QR code below or use the hyperlink to access the free workbook that will walk you through the process.

https://prfor.life/the-power-of-pr-parenting-login-page-qr/

CHAPTER 2

RITES OF PASSAGE: TRANSACTIONS, TRANSLATION & KIDDO COPYWRITING

In this chapter:
- Easing difficult transitions
- Teaching value
- Prepping translators for key communication
- Honing writing skills

Growing up, I was told by various elders, "Do as I say, not as I do."

You too? We all got our share of confusing mixed messages.

We heard the directions, but we mostly watched the demonstration before our eyes. If we were lucky, we inherently picked up some of the good and left most of the bad, emphasis on *most*.

In watching my three children grow and evolve, I see myself or Isaac, or a combination of both, in their expressions and approaches to social, academic, and work life. They've adopted some of our good and, I will admit, some of our bad.

Though our kids emulate us, they are also quick to point out that they are their own person. "I'm not you, Mom. I'm me."

Sometimes they agree with our practices, and sometimes they say, "That's for the birds." (Well, my words, their message.) We have to try to show them the way, though, even if they don't follow, right? It's part of the job description of parents.

I'm a PR person, so I borrowed a page from my own professional book to show them the way. I did so by regularly applying work approaches to something the kids could relate to and accept as part of a standard or natural process. From toddlers to teens, here are a few examples of how public relations practices were applied to three universal rites of passage.

Public Relations Practice: Creative Transactions

During my time in business, sometimes it has worked out better to barter rather than invoice for money. This was the case for one particular project. The client and I couldn't come to terms on the money, so we agreed on a barter. They sent me a really nice sound-system speaker for the living room, which totally thrilled Isaac. The value of the system met my expectations of payment for the services being provided, and I was happy that my husband was happy—so all good.

Now, let's consider the little ones who have an attachment to their pacifiers. This was gold to all three of my kids when they were babies. Yours too?

In Hebrew, the pacifier is called a *motzetz*, or a *tzetzi* for short, with a literal English translation of a "sucker". When it comes to the pacifier, I think we can agree that we are all a bit of a sucker, as this object often takes on a life of its own and rules the house.

If you are going to the park, a playdate, or anywhere else, DON'T leave home without it! And heaven help us if we can't find the *motzetz* at any given moment.

"*Tzetzi!!!*" (or perhaps, at your house, "*Binki!!!*"), our sweet babies will shriek in a pitch that could break glass when you may not be able to produce it after a few quiet requests that grow in levels of passion. Their language skills are limited at that age. So, a tantrum inevitably follows.

You've been in this movie before too, yes?

Spoiled brats? No.

According to Mayoclinic.org, *pacifiers may provide a source of comfort to infants and also assist in reducing the incidence of Sudden Infant Death Syndrome.*[1]

Eventually, however, the day arrives when it's time to say goodbye to the pacifier and end this overdrawn love affair, which will only lead to crooked teeth anyway.

As per a Delta Dental report, according to the Academy of General Dentistry (AGD), *pacifiers can harm the growth and development of the mouth and teeth. Prolonged pacifier use can cause changes in the shape of the roof of the mouth, prevent proper growth of the mouth and create problems with tooth alignment.*[2]

This same report notes that *the AGD recommends that children stop using pacifiers by age two.*[3]

But how? You can't just take it away. That would be too traumatic. You need to give them something in return. But what would be acceptable to them? Money doesn't mean much to a toddler, BUT value does. So, just like in a service-oriented business, when you can't agree on the cash, try the barter. Here's how it played out at our house.

When the time arrived, I took each of my three kids to the toy store for a barter exchange.

They were briefed in advance of what was to come in order to build excitement, as well as to give them time to think about what they wanted and prepare themselves for the permanent parting with their treasured pacifier.

They were invited to pick out their toy of choice within reason. Guy chose a packet of Pokémon cards. I think Noa Lee went for some version of a Barbie, and Maya opted for bubbles. Each paid for their choice of toy with their *motzetz*.

Of course, I had had a quick and secret discussion with the cashier to elicit her support with the charade and gave her my credit card in advance. She slipped it back to me when my child was distracted with receiving their new toy in a store bag to carry home.

They were as pleased with their exchanges as Isaac and I had been with ours when we received the speaker in return for public relations services. I was compensated for my work, and my kids were compensated for giving up their pacifiers in a way that thrilled them and redirected their attention. Their choice of toy was something tangible in their hands, and bartering was something they could wrap their heads around.

I didn't just take their beloved pacifier away any more than you would take something out of a baby's hand without handing it straight back to them or replacing it with something else to hold. Rather than having a trauma imposed upon them, they gave up their pacifier by choice, in seemingly full control of the situation.

In addition to the psychology of the exercise, it also taught my children the concept of value. The pacifier was worth something to them, and they traded it for something they considered of equal value. Rather than experiencing loss and suffering a short mourning period, they were empowered to barter and had their first transactional experience.

If you think this could work for you, first brief your child about the impending exchange about a week before "shop day".

Then throughout this week, with a smile and growing excitement in your voice, ask them periodically what toy they have in mind for the big day. This gives you time to help them build the necessary motivation for the exchange and gives them time to think about the exact toy they want.

Then, together with your child, either get online or go to the store. Perhaps they know exactly what they want. If not, gently suggest different choices that are within your budget, but without pressure. If they want something out of budget, just tell them that the pacifier payment works only with the toys you suggested—a lesson in affordability. The final choice is theirs—within reason—and the power, seemingly, remains in their hands from start to finish.

The formal exchange is made when they can see the toy with their own eyes, and you can place it in their hand in exchange for the pacifier. Make the exchange and congratulate them on their purchase.

If later on, they cry and plead for their pacifier, give them a big hug, remind them of their amazing transaction, tell them how proud you are of them for being such a big girl or boy, and redirect their attention to their new purchase.

I hope the barter exercise saves you a big headache, pleases your kids, and ultimately rids you and your child of the coveted pacifier.

Public Relations Skill: Translation

In international public relations, you work with people from all over the world and hear different languages in the process. We are lucky that English is today's accepted international language of business, science, medicine, art, music, and many other areas.

That said, knowing more than one language, or at least some keywords in the mother tongue of the person you are speaking with, like *hello, please,* and *thank you* and phrases like "Good morning, how are you?" can open doors, smooth otherwise rocky paths and make travel easier. It shows respect, that you are trying, and helps to break the ice, be it at the beginning of an executive meeting or simply when asking a stranger for help with directions or where to find the nearest bathroom.

In Israel, modern Hebrew is the main spoken language. You'll also hear Arabic and some level of English.

It was important to me that my children, raised in Israel and the United States, would be fully bilingual in Hebrew and English. There were four main personal reasons for this. Being bilingual would enable my children to:

- easily communicate and carry on an intelligent conversation with my side of the family and English-only speaking friends.
- translate for family and friends during an outing while they were visiting Israel.
- attend summer day, overnight and travel camp as well as school outside of Israel without a hiccup.
- be able to communicate with people from around the world, no matter where their travels took them in the future.

There are other intellectual advantages as well. As reported by CNBC, research published by Nature has shown that *bilingual kids are constantly switching between two languages in their brain and that this increases their "cognitive flexibility", the ability to switch* between thinking about different concepts or multiple concepts at once, and *"selective attention abilities"*, *the mental process of focusing on one task or object at a time.*[4]

The same study in Nature also showed that *adults who grew up speaking two different languages could shift their attention between different tasks quicker than those who pick up a second language later in life.*[5]

So, from the time of their arrival, for better or for worse, I was determined to raise fully bilingual children with translator abilities. Better: They have used these skills multiple times in different scenarios to their advantage over the years. Worse: As is the case with most young kids learning multiple languages concurrently, it took a little longer to perfect each.

Ours was an English household. I ONLY spoke and read to them in English. Isaac spoke to them in Hebrew when I wasn't part of the conversation. He would also read to them in Hebrew. However, most of their Hebrew language education came from out of the house during kindergarten, school, playdates, paternal family gatherings, and after-school activities, like ballet, judo, dancing, gymnastics, swimming lessons, music lessons, etc.

At the 8 a.m. drop-off to the kindergarten, they would be greeted with their nicknames.

"*Shalom* (Hello) GuyGoosh!"

"*Boker Tov* (Good Morning) Noa-Leh!"

"*Mah Schloh-mech* (How are you) Maya-Leh?"

For the rest of the day, they would interact with the other children and their teachers in Hebrew ONLY, as they ate their breakfast, lunch, and snacks, learned the lessons of that day, and played.

At 4 p.m., when Mommy arrived, they knew it was English time and would graciously translate for me.

A typical conversation would sound something like this:

"Hello, my gorgeous darling," I would say as I'd kneel down, with a bright smile to intercept my child running over to me with glee to deliver a big welcome hug. This is the best feeling, right?

I'd look up at the nursery or kindergarten teacher and ask, "How was the day?"

They'd reply in Hebrew something that might sound like this:

> "*Hayah lahnoo yome neyhedar. Guy tzeair tmoonah neyhederet, vegam seehaknoo eem hamahmterah. Ahchalnoo oogah leh aruchat arbah, avahl, Guy lo ohev oogah, az hoo zarak otah. Agav, nasoo bevakasha lehahgeeah mahar ba boker bahzmahn. Zeh Hashoov!*"

Jibberish, right? Not exactly.

(English translation: "We had a great day. Guy drew a wonderful picture, and we played in the sprinkler. We ate cake for the 4 p.m. snack, but Guy doesn't like cake, so he threw it out. By the way, tomorrow, please try to get here on time in the morning. It's important.")

My child, in this case, Guy, would turn to listen to his kindergarten teacher and then redirect his attention to me, "Mommy, she said we had a great day. Look at my picture! We played in the sprinkler. We had cake for our snack. Mommy, you know I don't like cake, so I didn't eat it. Oh, and she wants you to come on time tomorrow. It makes her mad when we're even a little late."

Translation and a little extra behind the scenes information. Thank you, Guy.

If we didn't have a late afternoon playdate or activity, then it was back home for English playtime. We'd dance to the best of Motown as well as hits from the 50s through the 80s and Broadway. Together, we watched Sesame Street tapes and lots of Disney movies. They LOVED the Winnie-the-Pooh beginners' reading computer games, where they practiced their ABC letter identification playing the honey-pot game.

The house favorite books included *Hop on Pop, Mr. Brown Can Moo! Can You?, Wish For a Fish, The Princess Who Never Laughed, Mouse Mess, Good Night Moon*, and the full series of Disney stories. When they were ready to take the plunge and start beginning reading, we started *I Can Read, I Can Read!* by Ilse Granoff.

Years later, in around 6th grade, Maya was invited to tutor English for a little girl in 3rd grade. Maya pulled the *I Can Read* book for these lessons. She had fond memories of this book, and it helped her to teach with confidence.

If my kids wanted something from me, they had to ask me in English; otherwise, no response. After all, Mommy doesn't understand or speak ANY Hebrew. (Wink, wink.)

In the beginning, it was all about spoken translation. Once they learned to read and write, it graduated to written translation and verbal translation of the writing as well, including report-card comments. Isaac would confirm or disconfirm the accuracy of their translations.

From nursery school straight through to today, my kids have translated for me. They have done this frequently enough that it is automatic. Practice, practice, practice.

I recently tested this. Noa Lee was addressing a group of 25 people at an army farewell party that our family attended. She began in Hebrew. The moment she felt me tap her shoulder, she accepted my cue and instantly switched to accent-free, American English.

All three are accent-free American English speakers. All three are proficient writers and have voracious reading habits. Amen, for e-readers, there isn't an extra space to stash even a piece of paper in our library at home. And all three can translate on the spot, verbally and in writing. These skills have not only proven useful in daily life but have also been sought out from a professional perspective.

At the conclusion of Noa Lee's graduation from her military course, I had a brief conversation with her commander. He couldn't tell me what she'd be doing, but I figured this question might get an answer.

"Will you be using Noa Lee's English skills?" I inquired.

"We're counting on them," he replied.

I smiled and said with a slight chuckle, "You are welcome."

I thought: *Mission accomplished.*

You too can bring up multilingual children, no matter in what country you may live. The earlier you start, the better. According to Parents.com, *It's best to introduce a new language in the first year of life. And if not, then it's best to wait until your child is about 2½ or until after they have undergone a "vocabulary explosion" in their first language, which generally begins at 18 to 20 months.*[6]

I have a stylish first cousin, who has lived in Mexico with her charming husband for the past 30 years. She sent her two children to a French School in her area. Today her beautiful children are grown and fluent and literate in French, English, Spanish, and I believe Italian too. Both automatically switch among languages and translate like the best of them.

If it's important to you, you can do this too. Just remember to be patient and consistent with whatever language training system you choose whether it be a school, a tutor, grandparents, yourself, movies, books, music, computer games, or a combo. And if possible, create a natural and appropriate situation that they will accept to learn this second, third or fourth language, and watch them shine.

Public Relations Skill (101): Kiddo Copywriting

Strong writing skills are a prerequisite for any publicist. Our talent and abilities in this area are constantly being tested and challenged as we try to brilliantly story tell a client's unique selling points (USPs), essentially, what makes them special.

Good writing skills are also crucial for several rites of passage growing up. For example, college and scholarship applications—the ability to clearly explain yourself and your vision can make the difference in achieving success.

As adults, good writing skills are also important for our careers and our personal lives. At work, you may have the most brilliant idea or witness the most amazing event, but if your ideas and findings are not documented in a way that can be understood, then your brilliance will be lost on others.

From a personal perspective, our writing skills are tested every day as we post on social media or text our family and friends with a greeting, a request, an update, congratulations, or a grievance. In all cases, we want our messages to be received and understood as intended.

Now, this doesn't mean we all need to have Shakespearean-level writing abilities, but we do need to up our game enough to deliver clear communication, and we can teach our kids to do the same.

YES, for some, this comes naturally, and for others, work is required, but indeed, good writing skills can be learned and improved with practice. My high school guidance teacher told me at the end of my junior year that I would never be a writer. And a university professor of Eastern European studies told me after the midterm exam that I write worse than a foreign student. In retrospect, this feedback makes me half-smile, given that I write and edit for a living today. But back then, I would say it was a negative motivator, and I was determined to prove the guidance counselor wrong (check) and impress my professor, which I managed to do with the final exam. He wrote on my paper: Well done!

It's never too early to start learning and practicing. At our house, the kids have been honing their writing skills from the very first visit by the tooth fairy.

According to the Mayo Clinic website, *A child's baby teeth typically begin to loosen and fall out to make room for permanent teeth at about age six.*[7] How convenient! This is around the same time the kids are beginning to learn how to write.

Our tooth fairy ceremony began with handwriting the tooth fairy a formal request letter, in English or Hebrew, sometimes both, depending on how far I felt I could push at the moment. Isaac or I would help them along the way with content as they requested.

Then, if the letter was in Hebrew, Isaac would edit it. If in English, then, with my child next to me, I would edit, in a soft, unalarming color (NEVER red), while explaining, "This is one way to do it. Let me show you another way."

I learned this approach from the former managing editor at what used to be KYW-TV News in Philadelphia. He was my copywriting mentor during my college internship there. Even when my copywriting was a disaster, the feedback was always positioned in the positive. I remember how empowered and inspired I felt after each editing session to practice more.

Following the edit, the kids would handwrite their letter again to make it "pretty" for the tooth fairy.

A letter could go like this:

"Dear Tooth Fairy,

My name is (fill in the blank). I'm (fill in the blank) years old. I know you work hard and are busy with lots of kids. If it's okay with you and you have time, I'd be very happy if I could receive money when you collect my tooth. If you don't have money, can I have some chocolate? Thank you very much.

Sincerely,
(fill in the name)."

I always tended to have chocolate in the house, which by the way, as per the ADA, *washes off the teeth more quickly than other candies. Dark chocolate (70% cacao) also has some health benefits.*[8]

Studies also show that *real chocolate is a good source of polyphenols, natural chemicals that reduce oral bacteria. Polyphenols also act as neutralizers on microorganisms that trigger bad breath.*[9]

With the letter complete, they would then fold it neatly, staple it shut, write Tooth Fairy on one side of it, put this letter into a plastic bag along with the coveted tooth, tie the bag closed and place the plastic bag with its contents under their pillow. Mission accomplished with pride and great expectations for the next morning.

A few hours later, when hopefully our child was in REM, Isaac or I would then go to our wallets in preparation for the big swap. Every once in a while, our wallets would be empty, and we would scour the house for enough loose change to make a reasonable payoff. Sometimes, we only had larger paper money, having just gone to the bank. Those were particularly thrilling years for the lucky kid.

"You gave him how much?" I remember asking my husband once.

"That's all I had," he replied, with a *What would you like me to do?* gesture.

We'd tiptoe into our child's bedroom, whisper their name to double check consciousness, slide our hand under their pillow, gently pull out the plastic bag and replace it with the money or, on the rare occasion, a chocolate bar, milk or dark, depending on preference. Then we'd scurry out, hoping they weren't faking sleep, which was the case on occasion as they got older. They tried to stay awake to meet the tooth fairy, suspecting she may not be the Tinker Bell-like fairy we had described.

"Mommy, is that you? I KNEW you were the tooth fairy!!!" Guy declared once in a sleepy, *I caught you* voice as he sat straight up in bed, brown hair tousled and hazel eyes bloodshot.

"Guy, I came in to grab a pen from your desk. Go back to sleep, honey."

Yes, I was snagged, but I tried to keep the faith going.

We continued this practice until Maya's last baby tooth fell out and far after they all understood that neither Mommy nor Daddy was the tooth fairy. It was an accepted ritual that honed their copywriting skills in a fun and natural way. Over the years, their letters became more involved and descriptive. And until today, it is a joy to find one of these letters when sifting through our "memory closet" for one thing or another.

I'd share these with you, but these letters remain a private conversation between my children and the tooth fairy.

All joking aside, I highly recommend kiddo copywriting exercises early on and whenever the opportunity arises, whether it's letters to the tooth fairy, some other imaginary icon, or thank you notes to friends and family. And when they get older—even their social posts and text messages are game.

Maya left this morning for a trip to a friend's house two hours away. She just sent me a WhatsApp:

"At her house and I eat food." Hmmmmm. Just a bad autocorrect?

I replied, "Please rewrite this and resend in proper English."

"I'm at her house. I had lunch already," she immediately texted back.

Perfect! Exhale.

Remember:

- Creatively reward your child for their efforts during difficult rites of passage
- Clear expression, and in multiple languages, is fundamental for your kids not just at school, but throughout their lives
- Make writing a fun time rather than a chore

If you would like to practice applying the public relations strategies above to your own story, please use your cell phone camera to scan the QR code below or use the hyperlink to access the free workbook that will walk you through the process.

https://prfor.life/the-power-of-pr-parenting-login-page-qr/

CHAPTER 3

PUBLIC SPEAKING & PRESENTATION

In this chapter:

- Presenting and performing in public with confidence
- Getting rid of the nervous energy
- Constructive critiquing
- Preparing key messages and talking points
- Planning events with executive thinking

I generally hate going to conferences and listening to people speak, mainly because most presentations are just plain old boring. Occasionally, someone actually holds my attention from start to finish.

There was a particularly wonderful speaker at one of the healthcare conferences in Tel Aviv one year. The speaker's important and conversationally-presented talk on healthcare reform was laced with a witty chronicle of Mick Jagger's career. I think that was the only time I laughed out loud at a medical conference and didn't zone out once.

Why are the majority of presentations boring? Here's a short laundry list of reasons:

- Nerves
- Overly sophisticated language
- Fear of not being taken seriously if the presentation includes a sense of humor
- Unfocused key messages
- Too fact- or statistic-concentrated
- Lack of storytelling
- Robotic-sounding delivery
- Longwindedness

Really now, it doesn't have to be this way.

It's important to share your brilliant ideas clearly and in a memorable way, otherwise your brilliance will be lost on the audience whether you are giving a presentation or an interview.

Here is how I train my clients to give a "good show", be the delivery dramatic, comedic, and/or action-packed and no matter how light or sophisticated the content.

Public Relations Practice: Defining Key Messages

Whether it's for a formal presentation or a media interview, we start by converting long and detailed explanations into clear and concise key messages.

Ask yourself, what exactly are the messages that you want to share with your audience? Next, what are the short stories that would support each of these messages?

Yes, it's recommended to throw a statistic or two in there to back up your thesis, just know that your audience will recall your stories way more than your statistics.

Next, practice delivering your stories in kindergarten-level language. This is not to say that the audience has a kindergarten level of understanding. The point is that when your presentation or interview is meant to be heard by the ear and not to be read by the eye, you want to choose words and a way of storytelling that can be easily understood and instantly processed the *first time* (do you remember the first time you heard the word *supercalifragilisticexpialidocious? What? Exactly!*) and within the designated time constraints. Do we have two minutes or two hours?

Consider the format of your presentation or interview. Is it in-studio on TV, on TV using video chat, in person in a small or big room, in person on a big stage, or by phone or chat for a podcast? Each format has a different frame of space for you to work with, or not, as in the case of the audio podcast, where sound is the only thing to worry about.

Small movements seem big when you are in a tight closeup on camera but might go unnoticed if you are in a huge auditorium or theater, where you have the opportunity to work the room and go bigger with what you do visually.

After a few run-throughs, begin recording your practices and watch the extremely important playback to see what you liked and what you want to change. You can also practice in front of the mirror. Watch your performance "live" and adjust real-time as you wish. Either way, ask yourself these questions: Did you like the story you told? Did it include your key messages? Were you conversational and animated? If the visual is important, does your body language add or subtract? Are you smiling? If on video, are you looking in the correct spot? Are you gesturing with your hands the right way?

Make *all* your mistakes during practice.

Then, an hour before you are to go on, it's time to get rid of the *shpilkes,* which is Yiddish for nervous energy. *Shpilkes* inevitably come with the buildup of adrenaline before an interview or presentation.

How do you get rid of your *shpilkes?* Find a private spot, even in a restroom, play your favorite music and, depending on your preference, dance, shake out your body or maybe just stretch and sing along. It's like a sorbet for the brain and helps to clear your head, get rid of some of that tension, and get your focus.

Now, you may be thinking. ARE YOU KIDDING ME? DANCE? SHAKE OUT YOUR BODY? IN THE BATHROOM? THAT SOUNDS **RIDICULOUS**.

Well, maybe so, but I can tell you with full confidence that this works. I know because this has been part of my media and presentation training techniques for decades, and all of my clients swear by it, from CEOs to scientists to industry leaders.

In some cases, I had weeks to train a client and sometimes only an hour. Regardless, I always tell or show my clients what I WANT them to do, rather than what I DON'T want them to do, which is a very efficient and successful approach when training professionals AND when teaching your kids.

I promise you one thing becomes clear after coaching so many different people, including my kids: We all know when we have messed up, even before we've watched the playback. The playback just gives us the specifics of what to change and keep.

Rather than wasting time with the negative, concentrate on the positive of at least something that was done correctly. If you are the trainer, demonstrate "another way to do" what the trainee should change for reference, and THEN—it's their turn again. With a positive example in hand, each subsequent round of practice is certain to be better than the one before, and your trainee might even start to have fun, which is crucially important. The more fun it is, the more your trainee will be inspired to practice.

Presentation as a Path to Self-esteem

Now, why is all of this important for parenting? And more specifically, why is this important for you and your kids?

There will be times in our kids' lives when they will be tasked with being in the spotlight. It could be a speech for a class or maybe even graduation, or an interview for college admission or perhaps a job. They are all important. Wouldn't it be great if they already had just enough experience and know-how to help them excel?

It doesn't matter if your kid is outgoing or shy. The spotlight changes things. With some level of confidence built from practice, encouragement, and guidance, you can prepare your kid for showtime. And if they trip up—all good. Encourage them to brush themselves off and try again, reminding them that sometimes we learn more from our hiccups than our successes. The goal is to build self-esteem and have a good time doing it.

Now that we know the *why*, let's get into the *how* to teach the kids.

A traditional event or rite of passage is a good place to start.

For example, in the Jewish religion, boys at 13 and girls at 12 years of age celebrate a ceremonial rite of passage from childhood to adulthood in what is called a Bar or Bat Mitzvah respectively. There is a religious ceremony in the synagogue usually followed by some type of party. I leveraged both opportunities to teach my kids *presentation* and *performing in public* skills. No matter your customs, you can do the same too with *your* ceremonies and associated parties. Same same. Different different.

During the Bar or Bat Mitzvah ceremony, the Bar or Bat Mitzvah traditionally gives a sermon at the conclusion. This speech generally connects the lessons from the Torah portion that day with some current event, and the Bar or Bat Mitzvah shares their opinion on both. YAY! Two in one: writing and analysis assignment. Thank you, Rabbi!

My kids prepared for and delivered their speeches in English so that our English-only speaking family and friends, who graciously traveled to be with us from abroad, would understand. (Again, YAY, English assignment!) As for our local Israeli friends and family, most people in Israel understand and speak a reasonable level of English. Israelis start learning English in the 3rd grade.

Let's break it down. In-person presentations to individuals and to groups are always best when they are not read, but rather delivered with direct eye contact and in a conversational format laced with stories. We've all watched people read from a page, right? I think we can agree that it's just plain old boring.

I advise my clients and my kids to begin with talking through and then documenting all of the points that they'd like to share in a first draft of their speech on paper or on the computer. Don't worry how good or bad it is written. You can edit and tinker to your delight after you get the ideas down.

After you are pleased with your edits, take your written speech and create a "cheat sheet", which includes both your key messages and the associated story for each.

From the cheat sheet, create a keyword paper that will remind you of your key messages, the relevant story for each, and in what order you'd like to share. If you need, hold this tiny piece of paper with the keywords for reference when you present. And don't worry if you mess up the word choice or order. It doesn't matter, as only YOU will know.

And yes, I practice what I preach, whether it's a one-on-one briefing, a formal presentation, an introduction of a keynote speaker, or an informal speech at a party. With the exception of the time I lost my voice the night before Maya's Bat Mitzvah and had to type my comments which Noa Lee read on my behalf, I have always either spoken with a keyword paper in hand or from memory. There were also times when I was invited to speak with only a very short time to prepare. In these cases, you just need to walk through the process in your head.

Here's an example of how to do this:

At Noa Lee's military goodbye party, I was asked to say a few words. I had nothing prepared, so a few minutes before it was my turn to speak, I defined my key messages in my head and decided on the associated stories I wanted to share:

- Thank everyone for their service
- Still don't know what Noa Lee did in the army
- Note the hints that didn't make any sense: what she brought home or left the house with on any given day
- Share Noa Lee's nickname along with a connecting story
- I love you, and GOOD LUCK

When my turn came, I hit each point and most of the stories I wanted to share. I missed one example, but, again, the ONLY one who knew was me.

I also tried to make it at least a little interactive by bantering with the audience along the way and including them in my presentation. I spoke conversationally at what felt to me was a snail's pace—really, REALLY slowly.

As I explain to my clients and my kids, speaking at a pace that you consider to be molasses slow gives you time to think about what you want to say next, helps to avoid stuttering, and enables your audience to absorb what you have to say the first time. Pumped with adrenaline, what seems slow to us, sounds normal to your listeners.

I can tell you with full confidence that this works. For example, one of my clients, a power gal scientist, spoke so quickly and with such fancy words when we started interview practice, it was challenging for me to understand her. So, I demonstrated speaking in excessive SLO-MO to her and in easy science terms, which I call Science-101.

Oh, how we laughed at my exaggeration of the SLO-MO! But the point was made, and she learned lightning fast. A few weeks later, she gave a brilliant, crystal-clear, five-minute, live interview on U.S. national television. Though she felt she was speaking painfully slowly, to the rest of us, she delivered like a star. Yay for her. Yay for the viewers. Yay for the proud PR Mama. To this day, she gives a fantastic, fully comprehensible interview explaining the applications of the company's sophisticated technology in Science 101 language that even kindergarteners could understand.

I am also giving you permission to deliver *pregnant pauses*, those longer spaces of silence, wherever and whenever you need. When you speak slowly, your audience will hardly notice a pregnant pause, if at all. Plus, it's much better than listening to a series of *ahs, ems*, and *ums* that you would naturally use to fill in the dead space when speaking quickly as you consider your next real words to say.

Now, at my kids' Bar and Bat Mitzvahs, Guy, Noa Lee, and Maya opted to have their full speech in front of them, like a security blanket. This is fine. Whatever works. That said, they knew their key messages and associated stories well enough that they maintained consistent eye contact with their audiences, spoke with loads of expression, and delivered their comments with wonderfully comic timing.

A highlight was Guy's congratulations speech to Noa Lee at the conclusion of her Bat Mitzvah ceremony. No notes.

He was 15 and dressed in a white shirt and dark dress pants, his short dark hair well-brushed. Guy stood next to Noa Lee, who was wearing a fluffy, light pink dress, her long brown hair flowing with curls. They faced the audience from the *bimah*, the podium separating the audience from the Torah Ark. He put his arm around Noa Lee's waist to his left, looked straight in her face, and declared (and this is a direct quote from the video recorded that day), "I want you to know that I love you and that you are the best sister I could ever have."

"And you too, Maya," he said in a lower voice, less than a split second later, with a turn of his body in the direction of his 7-year-old sister sitting in the front row.

Everyone laughed, including Noa Lee, who replied, "Don't say something you'll regret." Guy and Noa Lee hugged. The laughter transitioned into an *ahhhhhh*.

I wish this type of moment for all parents.

Fast forward five years. It's now Maya's Bat Mitzvah. In the interest of time, I typed her speech, which she dictated word for word to me. I didn't change a thing.

Maya never actually read her speech after I typed it. She, like her sister Noa Lee, is diagnosed as dyslexic.

Reading a text out loud can be challenging for someone who is dyslexic, so I didn't push it during practice as a way to carve the key messages into her memory, and you already know how I feel about presenters *reading* their speeches anyway.

On the day of Maya's Bat Mitzvah, the speech was in front of her on the *bimah*, but she never looked at it. She knew exactly what she wanted to say, and though the words may not have been exact—truly not important—the messaging remained *exactly* the same. YES!

Maya maintained full eye contact with our guests throughout her entire 10-minute remarks, shared interesting stories, and delivered her sermon with heartfelt intonation. She had our attention from start to finish.

Today, all three take the microphone with ease and deliver clever remarks conversationally.

Am I proud? Yes. Is this remarkable? No. You can teach yourself and your kids to do the same, too, by following the aforementioned instructions. Just remember to be patient with yourself and especially with your kids during practice, whether it takes hours, days, weeks or even months to get it right. The breakthrough will come.

Reminder: Do NOT criticize. This will only bum them out. They are already self-critical and likely already feel and know there's room for improvement, especially after they watch their playback. Rather, give them positive, proactive feedback so that they know exactly what to go for: "More energy." "Explain it to me like it's an everyday conversation." "Confidence!" "YOU tell ME. YOU'RE the expert."

You'll be amazed at how quickly they progress.

Performance

With the Bar or Bat Mitzvah sermon and ceremony behind them, it was time to party! We had a big lunch or dinner party for all three, where our Bar Mitzvah boy or Bat Mitzvah girl was center stage as the entertainment. It was big because both Isaac and I have large families, and everyone is ALWAYS invited. But remember, big parties don't necessarily mean big costs.

When planning for work or something personal, there is always a guest list and a budget. Both range in length and size. Set yours and stick with it. Isaac made me stick to ours.

I've organized swanky press breakfasts at the Four Seasons Hotel in Boston, where everything was posh, posh, posh. I've also hosted private gatherings at home where it was easiest to order pizza and salads or boil a pot of spaghetti and crack open a jar of red sauce, which is *my* preferred speed of cooking. If Isaac was around, the menu was always upgraded. But really, whatever your budget and whatever you do, it's all good. The idea is to at least *look* like you put some thought behind it and, most importantly, that everyone enjoys.

In terms of entertainment for the Bar and Bat Mitzvahs, I thought to myself: *Why do I have to hire an act when I have one at home? After all, it is my child's day, so why shouldn't they be in the spotlight throughout? Plus, if THEY are the entertainment, then it gives them an opportunity to hone their performance skills, perform in front of a friendly and supportive audience, and enhance their level of self-confidence.*

Choosing the Right Act

Guy was initially inspired to study hip hop from watching the first *Step Up* movie. He asked for lessons, and luckily there was one reasonably priced class taught in our neighborhood. Even though the students were mostly high school girls, Guy, then in junior high, chose to participate. Now that's commitment.

When Bar Mitzvah time came around, I asked Guy if he would be willing to perform at his Bar Mitzvah party. He agreed, but by then, the teacher had gone on to other opportunities. So, we looked for an alternative, and Isaac found a breakdancing troupe around an hour and a half away from our house.

A group of professional dancers practiced with the kids once a week for several months and the price was right, so we went for it. Guy LOVED every minute of the training and practiced regularly at home. I LOVED watching how happy he was going through the process. The final performance, which featured Guy with the troupe, was a big hit at his Bar Mitzvah party too.

Guy had set a precedent, so when Noa Lee's turn was around the corner she was already thinking what she'd want to do. At the time, we were into the American singing competition TV show *The X Factor*. We'd watch the competition weekly together as a family, so it was no surprise when Noa Lee declared, "I want to sing like I'm on *The X Factor*."

I thought to myself: *Hmmm, an X-Factor type production, well, it's doable, but on a way, WAYYYY smaller scale. And okay, she wants to give a concert—good thing the kid can carry a tune.*

The preparations began with the help of a reasonably priced singing coach in the neighborhood, who has perfect pitch and can listen to any song and then play it on the piano. Noa Lee chose her songs—*Leave It All To Me* and *Hallelujah*.

Noa Lee practiced all the time—during her lessons with the singing coach who accompanied her on the piano, at home in the living room, bedroom or shower, and in the car on the way to school. She, too, LOVED every moment of the preparation.

Now, the online version of the *Leave It All To Me* instrumental track was in Noa Lee's key, but the *Hallelujah* instrumental track was not. So, as a present, the singing coach recorded it in Noa Lee's key so she'd be able to sing it with pre-recorded accompaniment the night of her performance. Noa Lee had the star night she had dreamed of.

By the time it was Maya's turn, she already knew that a Bat Mitzvah performance was a family tradition. Like her brother, she was into hip hop. By then, there was a program in the neighborhood again. We asked her teacher to choreograph something special for Maya. They chose three songs together: *Uptown Funk, Can't Stop the Feeling,* and *Girl on Fire.* The net result was a seven-minute dance. Maya trained one-on-one with her teacher for around four months, and then the professional male backup dancers were brought in for the last three practices. We chose male backup dancers, rather than friends or adult female dancers, to ensure that Maya was the star of the evening. It also made it possible to add lifts to the choreography. Retrospectively, it was a great choice.

All three kids put on a good show. But what struck our guests the most was not the proficiency of their performances but the high level of confidence with which they performed. Plus, it was clear to all that the kids were having a blast performing, and our guests fed off of this enthusiasm. The positive energy was contagious.

It wasn't about being perfect—it never was. It was about the experience, learning something new, and having fun. If it weren't fun, I would have cut it instantly.

Now you might be saying to yourself: All of this costs money. Well, it can. But training doesn't have to be expensive. There are ways to reduce or even eliminate expenses.

If you are lucky, you have someone in your family who can volunteer their time. For about 30 seconds—well, not literally, but you know what I mean, Noa Lee had considered Eastern dancing, and my sister-in-law, who, at the time, was a professional Eastern dancer by night and a Ph.D. candidate by day, volunteered to choreograph and train her as part of her gift. Sounded great to me. But after a very short time, Noa Lee lost interest and decided she wanted to sing.

There is also the internet. Years later, Guy taught himself how to play the guitar, literally from free online videos. Indeed, there are all sorts of ways to slice this onion.

Whatever your child likes to do, encourage them to practice, practice, practice, and urge them to share their talent—at home, at a party or a public gathering, no matter how big or small.

Also, be prepared to manage a time commitment to chauffer, watch and cheerlead. As parents, we are the executive producers, and it's on us to oversee the process, keep all costs within the defined budget, and ensure that our children are learning and having a great time doing it.

Again, and this is really important: It's NOT about perfection, winning an award, or becoming professional. It's about enjoyment and strengthening self-esteem and poise. When it's fun, even if they are shy, with the right amount of practice and support, watch them slowly come out of their shell, gain confidence, and actually relish their moment in the sun.

Final thought: Have those smartphones ready to record every step of the way, practice through performance. You will be glad you did, and even if they don't admit it, your child will be glad too—especially when they are a bit older and have the perspective of distance. You've created a nice memory for them.

Event Planning

I LOVE event planning—whether it's for something professional or for something personal—and I've organized many events over the years.

I love the actual process as well as the very cool people I've had the privilege of working with and meeting, famous and not. It just charges my battery.

From a planning perspective, the process is the same, whether it's for a press breakfast for a statesman or diplomat, a press conference for a politician, an elected official or a company, a breaking-ground event headlined by a world leader, or a birthday party for a kid.

And, as I always say to my kids and my clients, "The better the pre-production, the better the production." So, most of the energy should be poured into the "before", so you can sit back, relax and watch it roll by smoothly "during" the show.

It boils down to a lesson in a specialized set of PR skills—how to executive think, plan, pay attention to detail, and execute. This can be applied to many initiatives in life, not only parties and events.

I used party planning, though, as a way to teach my kids this skill set, and you can too if you'd like. Here's how:

Pre-Production

We begin with executive thinking and working backwards.

1. First, go to the chosen location of your event, survey the site, even if it's your own house, then close your eyes (or not), and imagine how you want your event to look. What is the main attraction? Hold that thought. Take a mental picture. That's what you are going to create.
2. Think out of the box. Ask yourself: What's your superpower? What is your child's superpower? Cooking? Baking? Art? Playing an instrument? Languages? Impressions?

Making funny sounds? Chess? Gymnastics? Can you leverage any of these for you or your child to be the entertainment?

3. List line items of everything needed for the event accompanied by all relevant details. I usually document this on an excel sheet on my laptop.

4. Exercise good telephone and negotiation skills to order what is needed for the best price possible. Borrow where possible.

5. Exercise diplomacy to make friends with all of the people you've hired for your team.

6. Document in writing all verbal agreements, remembering if it isn't written, it didn't happen.

7. As everything you've ordered begins to arrive at your house before the event, like parting gifts for your guests at the end of the evening, put them in the designated party space at home. If you take them out to show friends and family, remember to put them back in their designated spot immediately so that you'll be able to easily find them the next time. Note: Not everything has to be ordered. You can also buy supplies and do it yourself.

8. In your calendar, mark all the appointments scheduled for the event as well as schedule reminder prompts in your calendar, so you don't forget that your appointment is soon.

9. Reconfirm with each member of your team that all is in order with their part of the event.

10. After all is in place, just before "showtime", have a look at how each item is placed in your venue and think if

everything is situated correctly in terms of composition and angles to take the best pictures or video possible. Change things around as required.

The better organized you are in terms of your thoughts, documentation, and your designated space for each element, the easier it will be to keep it all straight.

And if nothing else, your newfound organizational skills will make daily life less stressful thereafter. For example, if you get into the habit of assigning everything a home, you'll always be able to find your car keys. They'll be in the same place every time. Woohoo!

My kids have watched me in action over the years. They've looked over my shoulder as I was updating my excel sheet. They've overheard me coordinate activity by phone and video chat.

In terms of family affairs, we'd first discuss how they'd want their affair to look, and then the *must-have* items and what *wasn't necessary*. They all did their part as assigned, too—helping with calls, *blocking* their performances, and practicing—lots of practicing.

Sounds like a lot of work, right? It is. But, if something like this is in your future, I promise you, you can do it, even if you are the most unorganized person in the world. See it in your head, make your lists, delegate to your kids where possible and go for it, one line item at a time, with your kids in earshot or watching you.

Observing and training have served my kids well, and it can yours too. And then, when they are old enough, pass the baton. *Guide* them, but let them do it—do it ALL.

Today, all three plan their own parties. Generally, food, beverages, and games. I understand that the teens are still into truth or dare and drinking games. Some things never change. Peer pressure can be overwhelming and unnerving. So, we've also had the discussion about how if friends are truly friends, they won't push you to do something you don't want. We also encouraged our kids to walk away if the peer pressure is unbearable and if they can't walk away, then to "call or text me or Daddy and we'll come pick you up, no matter what time it is, no matter where you are."

I told them they can blame me for anything they want in order to get out of doing something they feel isn't right or that they just don't want to do. The worst they can call you is a mama's or a daddy's girl or boy. So what? Sticks and stones, baby.

Passing the Baton

It was around a year into the COVID pandemic when Noa Lee and a friend completed their military service and decided they wanted to organize their goodbye party at the beach. This is the same party I spoke of earlier when we discussed presentation skills. They asked me for help with finding a venue and the planning.

In a call with the two of them, going straight to the first task on the list above, I recommended they first scout out locations and take a night or two to outdoor bar hop on the beach, introduce themselves to the manager at each location and learn what the cost and deliverables were. This way, with their own eyes, they could see what their choices were. They did. Based on their scouting homework, they decided to organize the party *on* the beach rather than rent a venue on its edge, which made the best sense for their purposes.

Next, they visualized how their event would look and made their list of what was needed to create what they saw in their imaginations:

- Floodlights
- Sound system
- Microphone
- Electrical charger
- Two, fold-out tables
- Two big woven blankets so guests wouldn't have to sit on the sand
- Music track
- Menu of food and beverages
- Cups, plates, utensils & napkins
- Invitations & reminders
- Etc.

Noa Lee and her friend called and either rented or purchased what they couldn't access from our house or her friend's. The girls and some of their friends physically brought everything to the site and set everything up. Noa Lee's friend's mother made lots of delicious food. Isaac contributed to the menu too. And the girls provided the beverages.

It was a wonderful party!

Aside from helping with cutting the vegetables for the vegetable plate for around 20 minutes, I stayed out of the pre-production and the production of the party. Baton passed.

Remember:

- Leverage rites of passage and family events for opportunities to help your children communicate, express themselves, learn organization skills and explore their passions
- When you feel they are ready, step back and let your children take the reins

If you would like to practice applying the public relations strategies above to your own story, please use your cell phone camera to scan the QR code below or use the hyperlink to access the free workbook that will walk you through the process.

https://prfor.life/the-power-of-pr-parenting-login-page-qr/

CHAPTER 4

MAINTAINING GRACE

In this chapter:

- Responding live to curveballs
- Maintaining professionalism—always
- Leveraging contracts to turn around a bad situation
- Investing in imaginary "filtering" earplugs

In public relations, sometimes we win, sometimes we lose, and sometimes, the hopeless unexpectedly turns to hopeful.

Over the years, I've had many professional wins: securing exciting clients, placing articles in top-tier publications, and landing coveted spots on highly-rated TV shows.

And sometimes, even with the best effort, some initiatives just crashed and burned: I didn't land the client, the editor said "no," or the TV producer ignored my pitch.

There were also those dramatic times when a very uncertain situation turned victorious—the effort I wasn't sure would produce produced, or when a victorious situation turned unexpectedly sour, even horrific. It can happen, especially with live TV.

Case in point: On October 27, 1999, my client was two minutes into a live, in-studio interview in London on CNN, when the planned five-minute spot was preempted by coverage of a terrorist attack on the Armenian National Assembly, where several people were killed, including two from the country's political leadership. Instead of being happy with an amazing two minutes live on international TV and showing empathy for the crisis, the client was annoyed and really pissed.

Hard news always outweighs a feature in such cases, and there's only so much we can control.

So, we keep trying, knowing that the worst anyone can say is "no" and that eventually, someone may actually say "yes" and praying for more yeses than nos and for the show to go on.

Public relations is indeed a roller coaster ride. I suppose it isn't just public relations, though, it's also life.

From early on, we are taught to be good winners and losers, and to do what we can to turn the bad stuff around. Easier said than done. Right?

When we win, we want to boast. When we lose, we want to scream every profanity we can think of and instinctively bad-mouth the perceived villain in our story. And when things aren't going well, we just want to run.

But, and it's a big *BUT*, even if this is how we feel, no one likes a bragger, a drama queen, or a quitter. Plus, when we become parents, these victories, disappointments, and daily struggles are no longer only our own. Our children are watching us and mentally taking a page from our proverbial personal notebook on how one should behave during the race or after crossing the finish line, no matter where they place.

With this in mind, win, lose, or draw, do it with grace so your children have an example of how to do the same.

Not easy, you say? Of course not, but it's doable.

The Big Win

One of my biggest media wins was an interview for one of my clients on one of the highest-rated, national daytime talk shows in the U.S. I was extremely excited.

It had taken nine months from the time I cold pitched the producers with my idea until the segment aired. Working with the friendly and very professional producers was spectacular, and the entire experience was a big WOW. After watching the segment, it was finally time to exhale and celebrate.

First, I did my PR "YES" dance. I held my arms slightly bent in front of me and moved them in rhythm from left to right, then right to left, my body following my self-defined beat. I chanted with a huge smile on my face, "uh huh, uh huh." The kids were in the living room at the time, and smiled and danced along with me, understanding how big it was for me and my client.

Then that weekend, it was off to one of my favorite spots, the lowest place on earth, the Dead Sea (422 meters or 1,385 feet below sea level). Isaac, our daughters (Guy was studying), and I floated in the salty water and covered ourselves in therapeutic mud from the bottom of the sea, which we grabbed with our hands in clumps.

It was stifling hot, so after our float, we relaxed under a canopy sipping alcohol-free, iced drinks and indulging in watermelon and, okay, okay, full disclosure, deep-fried French fries sprinkled with salt that we dipped in ketchup.

We all enjoyed, but without going overboard. And rather than shout to the world about my accomplishment, I chose to pay tribute on social media and in emails to the deserving client, producers, and show host. The accolades were reciprocated. The congratulations flowed in.

The lesson: Acknowledge your wins privately with your version of the "YES" dance. Celebrate the moment in the most satisfying way for you, even if it may seem "unglamorous". Your kids have a front-row seat to your journey and all the ups and downs along the way, so they have every right to join in the celebration. Finally, publicly thank and congratulate those who were key to making the win happen.

Win with grace and class.

Crash and Burn

I was walking the dog behind our house on the promenade, which hugs a nature reserve adorned with green trees and bushes and the remains of ancient agricultural terraces on the banks of a *Wadi* (meaning "valley" in Arabic and used in Hebrew) left over from communities from thousands of years ago.

It was around 5 p.m. Israel time, 10 a.m. on the East Coast of the U.S. The sun was still in the sky. My mobile phone rang. It was a friend and former client. I had worked with him several times at different U.S.-based companies. He had always invited me to join wherever he went professionally.

Very excited, he told me that he had an idea for a new company, explained the concept, and asked if I would help him by creating a mock website to show the possibilities of his idea to potential investors. I believed in my friend and thought the idea was fabulous. So I helped for six months, free of charge.

The effort was a success. Financing was secured, as was a contract for me, with a handsome enough retainer that, at one point, I even decided to make this initiative my sole focus. As I understood it, the plan was to grow the company into something big, really big. I was excited and all in.

I poured my heart into this job, and I loved every minute. We had a great team, and we were enjoying a continuous stream of all kinds of successes, including press. The future looked bright. At least, I thought it did.

One evening, after dinner my time, my friend, and then my only client, and I were catching up on action items—at least, this was on my agenda for the call. As I was going through the list, he stopped me.

"Marjie, this is one of the hardest things I've ever had to say, but I have to give you notice," he said with a strained and pained tone in his voice.

"What?" I screamed full volume with anger. So much for grace.

I was standing in front of the dining room table, still covered with dinner dishes and glasses. My kids and husband were either sitting or standing in the living room. The TV was lit with the evening news.

He understood my reaction and the short angry rant that followed. I know he had fought for me, but the investor had put his foot down: immediate, one-month notice, even though I only had six weeks left in my existing contract. It was also just after Isaac had returned home from his 10-day stay at the hospital, including five days in the Cardiac ICU. I thought: *cold and heartless, but message received.*

It was also just a few weeks before the COVID-19 pandemic shut down Israel, along with the rest of the world. Not a great time to be looking for new work. According to the World Economic Forum, 114 million people lost their jobs in 2020 due to the pandemic or the lockdown.[10]

My friend and now former client calmly replied, "Take some time to absorb this, and let's talk in a few days." We hung up.

My family had overheard the entire conversation. All eyes were on Mommy, and I knew it. I thought: *Oh my, this really sucks. I have no income. They are all staring at me. I have to show them that everything will be okay and, good grief, now I have to teach them how to fail with dignity. But how?*

I stood still for a moment in silence before quietly walking up the two flights of stairs to my bedroom. I closed the door and laid on my back, across the length of my bed, head on my pillow, staring out my window in the direction of the *wadi*.

I cried for a few moments and then just laid there in silence alone, fuming, until, after about ten minutes, I wasn't alone or fuming anymore. One by one, my children knocked on my door, hugged me, and asked me if I was okay. I knew I had done something right as a parent for them to be so proactively and demonstratively sensitive and caring.

I said, "Yes. I am okay." I had taken my self-designated ten minutes to feel really badly about it and then closed the door on that chapter. I told myself: *Enough! Yallah*, meaning *Let's go*, or *Come on* in Arabic and used in Israeli slang.

I explained to my children, with the weight now lifted off my shoulders, because after all, it's all about our attitude, "Job schmob. They come, and they go. There will be others. Let's get on with it." Yes, those were literally my words.

So, that's what I did. I quickly moved on, with as much grace and class as I could gather, head held high, as an example for my children, who exhaled when they understood that I truly was okay.

A week later, I spoke to my friend and former client again, this time with composure, and formally closed this chapter.

If you have recently lost your job for whatever reason, pandemic or otherwise, know that it's a temporary situation. You will find another one and perhaps an even better one. Take ten minutes to feel like crap, then take a deep breath and move on, head held high, knowing that you rock and that you will be an asset to the next company lucky enough to hire you. This positive energy will give you strength, provide your children with much-needed sunshine and assurance and catapult you forward.

The Redirects

I have a general rule: No written contract, no public relations services.

I have made exceptions here and there over the years, like when helping out a friend or volunteering to give back to the community. But if you want to keep things clean and avoid any "stickiness", I highly recommend that you document your agreement to avoid any misunderstanding.

Determine what your value is and negotiate for that, or even more, so that after the handshake or elbow bump, and the signing of the contract, you can forget about it, and feel good about doing your job.

I also don't provide PR strategies or plans in advance of being put on contract. I did this twice, separated by two decades, and both times, the potential client took my ideas and implemented them on their own.

And, even when there has been a contract, there have been times when clients delay payment or threaten not to pay at all. This has also happened a few times over the years and has always required the self-confidence and *chutzpah* ("nerve" in Yiddish) to respectfully confront the client.

I had several kind but firm conversations using the "I-message". It's a friendly way to approach a sticky situation and elicit compliance: "I'd like to resolve this as quickly as possible. I'm willing to be a little patient, as I would prefer to keep a good relationship with you and not have to go to court."

Luckily things worked out, and I didn't have to sue any of my clients. But crap, I was annoyed and furious. I thought: *Heck, I have to feed my kids with the money you owe me. And now I have to exhaust all kinds of energy, I should be putting elsewhere, to run after you? Who needs this kind of aggravation? Why couldn't you just do what we had agreed on? I did.*

Best to avoid the "he said, she said" thing. It just doesn't work. It is extremely important to document in a contract all expectations, promises, deliverables, compensation, and consequences. Otherwise, you don't have a foot to stand on if the other person doesn't come through. And if they don't come through, then it's time to see the judge with your proof of agreement in hand.

There were also broken promises in situations where I should have insisted on at least an email confirmation. I was working at a PR agency when my direct manager at the time promised me that he'd back me for a promotion and a raise at my review. When the time came, sitting with all the top management, he sat quietly, saying nothing, and smiled and nodded at the others, who congratulated me on a job well done but offered no raise or promotion.

My anger overshadowed my fear to confront him after the meeting.

"What happened," I asked perplexed. "Did you change your mind?"

"No," he said sheepishly. "I still think you deserve the raise and promotion, but as you can see, in that meeting, I towed the company line." ASSHOLE!

I didn't have anything in writing from him documenting his promise, so there was nothing to do about it. He had lied to me. No consequences. He got away with it, smug smile and all.

This was not going to happen again to me at work or at home. At least, I promised myself I would do what I could to avoid it. And you can too!

Life lesson: We can only do what we can do, and we can only change ourselves, not others. For these reasons, don't rely on verbal promises. Create and document situations that will give you your best chance possible at a happy ending.

So, how does all this translate into parenting?

I was editing a scientific press release announcing the findings of a clinical study in my small office on the first floor of our house. Though it was towards the end of the workday, there was still light streaming in from the window on my right, facing the plum tree and jasmine vine woven around the iron railing in our front garden.

I was deep in thought when my mobile phone rang. The number displayed told me it was Guy's junior high school teacher.

"Hi. What's up?" I asked.

"I'm sorry to tell you, but Guy has been skipping class," she explained in a friendly but concerned tone in slightly Israeli-accented English.

Guy was a good kid, a smart kid. He attended one of the top semi-private schools in the country. This is the kind of school that requires an entry test and interview to be accepted and provides all kinds of extra-scholastic opportunities.

I accidentally learned from a fellow working mom about the existence of this school the night before the entrance exam. I called the school the morning of the test to see if they could squeeze Guy in. They could. That afternoon, I picked Guy up from elementary school, handed him a pencil and a candy bar for quick energy, and said, "Go for it. If it works, great. If not, nothing happened. All good. No pressure."

Guy has always been a very easygoing and just *roll-with-it* kind of kid. He is also well-mannered, polite, and on the quiet side. He loves sports of all kinds and is mostly a self-taught musician. He plays the guitar and the piano and writes and sings original songs. He even studio-produced one of them after he finished the military. Guy has also always been a voracious reader. I didn't think I had anything to worry about. We talked every day. I thought he told me everything. I was wrong.

I couldn't believe what the teacher was telling me. A shock of electricity ran through my body. I paused for a moment to absorb the information and immediately went into mama bear protective mode.

"Are you sure? Maybe the teacher with all those kids just missed him?" I suggested, still dazed by the news.

I had seen him every morning before he left for the 7th grade. And he always came home at the anticipated time.

"Marjie, he skipped a midterm exam too," she explained matter-of-factly.

I thanked the teacher for bringing this to my attention and promised I would speak to my son.

More confused than anything, I asked Guy about the accusations. I expected an honest answer. He looked me straight in the eyes and flatly denied it all. I believed him and tried to figure a way to resolve what I thought was a gross misunderstanding.

About a week later, for reasons I don't know, Guy finally came clean. He had been skipping for six weeks. He was hanging out with the "popular kids" at a park near the school. He insisted they weren't doing drugs or drinking alcohol, just hanging out. So why?

He explained, "I loved the freedom of skipping school." He found that quite intoxicating to the point where this went on as long as it did until the teacher finally flagged it. I wish the teacher had called me earlier.

I was in my pajamas in bed, ready to go to sleep, when my husband declared the truth of the situation to me. I instantly broke into tears, sobbing so audibly, I'm sure the neighbors down the block heard me. Forget the skipping for a second, my son had lied to me. I was devastated.

Well, guess what. Kids lie. Well, maybe some don't, but many do, but not because they are bad. They just don't want to get into trouble. At least, this is one of the reasons.

I thought my kids would never lie to me. I thought we had a solid trust and open communication where they could tell me anything. I always reminded them that if there's a problem, I can only help if they tell me the truth. I wanted to trust that our verbal agreements were sound. And in most cases, they were, but when they weren't, they *really* weren't.

There were the big infractions like regularly skipping school, and there were the little ones like agreeing to do something that wasn't done, from cleaning up their room, to walking the dog, to completing and submitting homework to a teacher, to updating where they might be at a certain time, to arriving by the set curfew of the day. Good, smart kids sometimes do silly, and let's be honest—*stupid* things.

Isaac and I were called in once to the high school in our neighborhood to face what felt like an inquisition. We arrived at a small, dimly lit, generic room, where a team of four senior educators sat in hard office chairs aligned in a half circle. We took our seats across from them.

This time, we were informed that *Noa Lee* had been repeatedly skipping school. They had thought to call social services but refrained knowing that we are a good family.

The senior educator in the room asked me, "Do you know where she is during the day? Do you know what she's doing?"

Yup, I knew where Noa Lee was—at home, in her bed, with her eyes closed, blinds down in her dark room, hiding from the light and complaining of a terrible migraine. In dramatic performances worthy of an Academy Award, Noa Lee would declare that she was suffering and just couldn't go to school that day. The problem was this was the rule, not the exception to the rule, and she had missed, I don't remember how many days of school.

If you have a teen, my guess is that you have been a main character in some version of this movie too. So you get me, right?

I looked at the head educator and replied, "She's home, in a dark room, with her head glued to her pillow." I suffer from horrible migraines too, and sometimes there's just not enough over-the-counter extra strength pain killers in the world to get the job done. So, I was sympathetic, maybe too much so.

I continued, "When she was little, I could pick her up, throw her in the car, and insist on attendance. She's taller than me, and I don't have the physical ability to pick her up and throw her in the car like in the old days. You are welcome to come to our house and try that if you'd like."

The educators all broke into a half smile. They understood my point, and we all agreed to have separate talks with Noa Lee.

Yes, Noa Lee suffered from migraines. But the inherent problem was that she was bored and had lost interest. She had picked 11th grade, the most important academic year in terms of tests required for college applications, to rebel and not show up. I hadn't realized just how many days she had missed.

I also wasn't aware of the enormous discontent between Noa Lee and her chemistry teacher, which was also brought to my attention. Noa Lee had been insistent that she handle her own business and that her father and I stay the heck out of it, whatever "it" was.

The entire issue crescendoed when Noa Lee decided to remain in chemistry and take the final after telling the teacher weeks earlier she was leaving to study biology. Things didn't work out as Noa Lee had planned, and at the last minute, she decided to stick with chemistry.

In earshot of us, she left a voice message on the teacher's answering machine to this effect the Friday night before the Sunday morning final. Enough was enough. Isaac was insistent that I take care of matters.

On the morning of the final, dressed in full professional wear rather than my usual casual wear, I accompanied Noa Lee to school to make sure she took the test. The teacher was livid when she saw us standing at the entrance to the science lab, started screaming at us and waving her attendance chart in our faces, pointing out all of Noa Lee's skips.

She insisted on speaking with the head-of-the-class teacher before she'd give Noa Lee the test. It was 7:30 a.m. The test was to begin within the hour.

I managed to get the head-of-the-class teacher, who had yet to arrive at the school, on my mobile phone, which I handed directly to the chemistry teacher standing in front of me, now in the hallway outside of the classroom where the test was to be given. After a two-minute conversation, the teacher reluctantly agreed to give Noa Lee the test.

I watched Noa Lee enter the classroom and sit at a desk, with the closed test on the desk in front of her. I left the classroom, closed the door behind me, slid onto the bench in the hallway, and deeply exhaled. OY VEY. It was an exhausting ordeal, but mission accomplished—she was taking the exam.

Contracts with Your Kids

It was my mother's idea to have the kids sign written contracts, just like I insist on at work, documenting the expectations and the consequences in the event expectations were not met, like showing up to school. My mother is a licensed clinical social worker (LCSW) and the one who regularly reminded us growing up, "If it isn't written, it didn't happen."

All three of our children chose the consequences (approved by Isaac or me) that would be imposed for the current infraction as well as any similar ones in the future. The kids signed their contracts. Isaac or I countersigned the same.

Advice: Try to agree on a consequence that you can enforce as a parent, otherwise your kid won't take this seriously. And ONLY take away privileges, big or small, but NEVER basic life needs, like food, liquids, a place to sleep, the roof over their head, or your love. They may need a big hug now more than ever, all things considered, when caught doing wrong. Remember, they are good kids, who just made a stupid mistake. We all make mistakes. Show me someone who hasn't.

BUT, if the terms of the contract are broken, you need to dig deep to find the strength to follow through and hold your ground. There were times when Isaac and I just didn't care if we were popular at home. It's nice to be friends with our kids, but in my opinion, being the *parent* is the more important role.

A contract could look like this:

> I, (name of the kid), agree to (name the expectation—attend class, do my homework, clean my room, etc.). If I do not (name the expectation) in the future, the following penalties will be implemented and enforced:

- *Grounding for a week*
- *No screen time from 4 - 10 p.m.*

(Kid's signature)
(Parent's signature)

For the record, Guy was grounded for a full month, yes for skipping school and the midterm, but mostly for lying. Over-the-top offense: over-the-top consequence. Noa Lee was also grounded from attending parties for a short time following her attendance and chemistry mess. Even though they had both skipped, Noa Lee hadn't lied, so her consequence was lighter.

During our conversations, the kids were invited to explain their sides of their stories (which can be very illuminating), and then, after listening, we would explain ours. Between the contracts, the enforcing of the contracts, and, most importantly, the dark rainclouds hovering over their heads from the overall crappy experience, the big questions were now: Will they redirect? And how will they do it?

Well, Guy and Noa Lee both redirected in a BIG U-turn and went from the proverbial zero to hero in the eyes of the teachers within a matter of months.

They had brushed themselves off, taken a deep breath, held their heads high, and with grace and dignity, managed to turn losing scenarios into winning ones. Their attendance was now perfect (aside from when they were actually sick), and their test scores impressively improved.

The veteran teacher of the class where Guy had skipped class AND the big midterm commented that in all of her years of teaching, she'd never before seen such a quick turnaround from any student. And the chemistry teacher wrote on Noa Lee's first-semester, senior year midterm that she had graded 100%, "Where were you last year?" Noa Lee was a new favorite and asked to write the class tribute to the chemistry teacher in the senior yearbook.

Today, Guy and Noa Lee have completed their mandatory military service and are currently studying at university.

Guy is studying for a BS in computer science and statistics at a prestigious university, and Noa Lee is studying to be a medical doctor at one of the top medical schools in the world.

It was very exciting to see both Guy and Noa Lee achieve their university goals. The lessons from chapters 1-4, including contracts, had served their purpose well.

Staying the Course

You can type or handwrite contracts. It doesn't matter. Bottom line: The kids need to know that you are serious, that they are accountable, and that you will follow through, no matter their age, and, no matter how much they carry on, scream, and shout. If it gets to be too much, invest in an imaginary set of earplugs, emphasis on the *imaginary*, to filter their dramatic temper tantrums.

These have always come in handy whenever I am fielding an angry client or public call. Filtering is key, at least for me, to focus strictly on the grievance and to reply thoughtfully, with respect, calm the situation and then do what I can to help. I listen to the core of the discontent and use my imaginary earplugs to filter raised voices, mean words, and aggressive deliveries.

I try to apply the same approach at home when addressed in high volume or rude language for one reason or another. For example, I use my imaginary earplugs to adopt a calm state of mind in the face of mega drama, listen to my child's key message of complaint, and respond to the grievance, not the dramatic performance.

On the flip side, the imaginary earplugs also helped when the kids were little, and they and their playdates got a little too loud while having fun. Naturally, I didn't want to spoil the fun, so the imaginary earplugs came in handy. One of my younger sisters, a physical therapist and the mother of four, and I used to joke that there was a *2-for-1* sale at the pharmacy and to make sure to stock up. To this day, if the screaming kid on an airplane isn't mine and I can't be of use, I can generally tune out the drama, imaginary earplugs in place.

Final Thought

Contracts will empower you, establish a sense of order, and give your kids some much needed boundaries, which, in some cases, are a way to show that you care. Do your best to hold your temper and find the power to stand up to your kids if they are being particularly rude and tend to walk all over you. Communicate with respect but with full, *take control* confidence, just like in the PR world when your client is misbehaving. This will help your kids to take their first step on a new and more promising path and, hopefully, with grace and class.

Remember:

- Your kids are watching, so lead by example—in the good times and the bad
- Remember that all kids do stupid things; it doesn't mean they are stupid
- Set guidelines and document terms in writing, at the office, and at home, especially when the issue is important
- Invest in imaginary "filtering" earplugs

If you would like to practice applying the public relations strategies above to your own story, please use your cell phone camera to scan the QR code below or use the hyperlink to access the free workbook that will walk you through the process.

https://prfor.life/the-power-of-pr-parenting-login-page-qr/

CHAPTER 5

KEEPING YOUR COOL

In this chapter:

- Managing yourself before you manage your kids
- Zooming in on those key messages (again)
- When in doubt, look to a mentor
- Helping, not handling

During the five years I worked for a PR agency, whether big or small, my working space was always in an open room, in community with my colleagues.

At the big agency, I think we were up to ten people sitting in the long, rectangular-shaped second floor of the building. My cubicle was just beyond the top of the stairs that led out to the middle of our fishbowl. The idea was that when clients would arrive at the "work room" after their one-level climb, they'd be excited by the hum of the room and the action in front of them.

It made sense. The room was always action-packed, kind of like the trading floor of a stock exchange before automation.

Everyone was busy drafting or editing, talking on the phone to clients or journalists, as well as researching or strategizing.

Yes, it always *appeared* that something special was going on. And more times than not, there usually was.

As thrilling as this all might sound, it also meant that the room was noisy.

Most of the time, I could tune out the work white noise—my colleagues making their magic. There were two colleagues, however, who spoke so loudly that they inevitably broke my concentration every time they picked up a phone or addressed a colleague.

This happened regularly enough that to say I was frustrated would be an understatement. I'd have my groove on, and BOOM, just like that, my concentration bubble would burst as abruptly as when you stick a needle in a fully blown balloon and, frankly, just as loudly.

What could I do? Respectfully complain? No. Both were company favorites, and no matter how nicely I would have said it, I was fairly certain that I would end up insulting someone. There was also the possibility of backlash or, even worse, receiving an invitation to leave if I couldn't handle the noise.

Maybe you can relate? Perhaps we all have that person or persons in our work environment, yes?

So, what did I do? I tried to turn these interruptions into a plus rather than a minus and used them as a natural time to get a coffee, get some air outside for five minutes, use the restroom, or go to lunch, whatever.

When I opened my own shop and started working from my office in my home, I thought it would be quieter. Not exactly.

In the very early hours of the day, the birds in the nature reserve behind our house usually come to order in their daily congress, all tweeting at the same time, in the birdy version of the Israeli Popolitica TV show where everyone screams over each other at the same time. During the day, there might be noise from a neighbor's house under construction or renovation, or from the kid next door shooting hoops in his front garden. In the later hours of the afternoon, there was the usual activity, plus the requests and the disputes to be refereed for my kids.

As they got older, the picture remained much the same and even got a bit crazier with the onset of the COVID pandemic. Due to the movement restrictions, the kids and Isaac were always at home, doing their academic or professional thing remotely. The good news was that I had my family near me. The challenging news: My workspace was no longer my own.

No matter what the reason, the various interruptions, inside and outside of the house, always seemed to come when I was in the middle of working out a thought or was just about to finish something for a tight deadline.

Even the dog has terrible timing. As I am writing this chapter, Rocky, our tiny Maltese with a high-pitched bark that could shatter glass, just asked me to open the door to the garden so he could go out.

I did.

We both know who's boss.

My internal reaction to each interruption is generally the same. Frustration, annoyance, and high anxiety, especially if a deadline is quickly approaching.

What did I do? What do I do?

I approached the kid next door, shooting hoops with a smile, and asked for a defined amount of quiet time to finish what I was working on so I could make my deadline, with only my internal stress to deal with. He graciously agreed. After that first talk, all I had to do was peek over the fence with a smile and say, in

Hebrew, of course, "*Schlosheem dahcote bevakasha?*" Translation: "Thirty minutes, please?" He would smile back and, again, in Hebrew, say, "*Ain bah-yah.*" "No problem."

Since there was nothing I could do about the construction during daylight hours, I'd do something that didn't require *pin-drop quiet* concentration, like cleaning my inbox, organizing my files, choosing images for a project, or returning emails that only required a short response. However, if I had a deadline so close that it felt like the sand was slipping way too fast through the hourglass, I'd put in those imaginary earplugs (they really do come in handy) and make my best effort to transform the screeching sounds of the construction drills into white noise in my brain.

Yup, distractions and concentration breakers are present wherever we are: at the office and at home.

Public Relations Skill: Managing Yourself First

It took a little while, but eventually, I adopted the same policy at home as at the agencies. To this day, if my concentration balloon is popped, I try to hold my temper and turn the disturbances into positives. Cool, break time with the kids!

When the kids interrupt, though, there is always the possibility that something really might be wrong, like a medical or safety emergency. For this reason, I always pick up the phone when my child calls me during a client visit, and I always stop what I'm doing if a child walks into my office, even if during a work video meeting. They know they need to be quiet during video meetings, so if they appear, my right eyebrow raises with concern.

If appropriate, I interrupt the work discussion, apologize to my colleagues, and excuse myself for a short moment before muting. If not appropriate, I just mute. Then I ask my child if it's a life-or-death emergency. If it's not, I say, in the most tender voice I can muster, "My love, I'm on a work call. As soon as this is finished, I'll be glad to help you." Then I unmute and return to the call.

The tone of voice I try to use with the kids is the same tone of voice that I use when I'm handling a fiery call from a journalist, a client, or like during my days at the Israeli Consulate, a caller with a complaint about a government policy. No matter whether I agreed or disagreed with the assessments of any of those on the other end of the line, and no matter how loudly they'd scream at me, I just had to deal with the tidal wave of negativity breaking above my head.

Even if I wanted to, I couldn't scream back any more than I could lose my temper with the loud people at the agency. This wasn't about staying calm, and it wasn't the same kind of situation like when Isaac collapsed. The lesson here is different.

In short, in any customer-service relations, we're always told to be courteous and respectful, for good reason, even if we feel like telling someone off or punching them out. Now, if we know this to be true at work, then when the kids interrupt whatever we are doing at any given moment, shouldn't we give them the same courtesy and respect and even consider their inquiries *more* important? After all, they are our babies.

Yes, easy to say, hard to do. How to pull this off?

There are times when one or more of my children will interrupt a video call, and instead of taking a moment to acknowledge them and defer their issue, I'll invite them to say hello to my colleagues, depending on the relationship with the client. These moments have tended to be appreciated by both my children and my client, who usually understands I'm a parent first.

In one case, Maya was in the target demographic for the consumer product my client was marketing. My client asked if Maya would be willing to try out the product and share feedback. Maya agreed and gave her unfiltered opinion. Guy also participated and offered his perspective as well.

Most times, though, when asked about something they clearly knew nothing about, my children would understand they were in over their heads and that it was time to exit left and to let us get on with our meeting.

Mind you, I don't invite my children to pop onto calls with everyone and certainly not regularly, but when they are invited, my children feel included in what I'm doing at the moment, as well as seen and not brushed off. Also, once they are in the spotlight on a video call, my children understand, in a crystal-clear but loving way, that now is not the time to bother Mommy.

Props and Mediation

In the early years, when my kids were in kindergarten and at the start of elementary school, I would ask them nicely, in a low volume, once or twice, to quiet down and define the length of silent time I needed until they could be noisy again. By the third time, I stepped up my game. In my best witch voice, I'd threaten to fly on my broomstick if they didn't behave.

Once or twice for demonstration, I held the top of the broomstick closest to the bottom of the brush with my hands, straddled the pole between my legs, put on my pointy black witch hat that I had bought at a toy store one year for Purim (a Jewish holiday where you dress up in costume, like on Halloween in the U.S.), threatened to fly around the living room and then let out a big, loud witch's cackle.

For some reason, the thought of me turning into a witch before their eyes, like the one in the Snow White animation, and flying around the living room on my broomstick really freaked them out. So, the response each time when I threatened to get my broomstick would be:

"No, Mommy! NOT the broomstick!"

Good thing the kids didn't call me on it, as clearly there was no way to follow through with my mortal props, and luckily, I got away with the performance.

I giggle to this day when I think of this and still call my broomstick my favorite form of transportation when explaining to clients that, if necessary, I will be tough not only on their behalf with the outside world to achieve a goal but also with them, like when I'm media training, so that they can be the best that they can be.

There were also those times when the kids did something or said something so over the top that I simply had no words and would respond with only a facial expression, like raising my right eyebrow, or an *Oh My Lord* or *You've got to be kidding me* look.

Sometimes, I'd gesture. No, not "the bird". More like a wave of my arms in the air to the sides of my head or a shrug of my shoulders. I've learned, assuming full eye contact, that this silent communication has the potential to be light years more effective than any amount of screaming. It worked well in professional meetings too, when body language spoke more clearly than any words I could summon.

I let a lot of things slide by too, without any reaction, like when my kids would make a snarky comment or when they would try to pick a fight with me. Sometimes, depending on your situation, as everyone has their own particular bag of potatoes to deal with, the best reaction is no reaction.

It's impossible to fight with a wall. You can scream all you want at a wall. It will never scream back. So, there were times, and certainly more than a few over the years, when I'd put in those wonderful imaginary earplugs AGAIN and pretend to be a wall until the temper tantrum ran its course and quiet returned.

Speaking of quiet. When was the last time you had a full night of quiet? For parents, these are few and far between. When they are little, almost never, between the feedings and the rest, right? When they are older, the fun takes on a whole new dimension.

One night, just before midnight, Isaac and I were woken up from a deep sleep by a loud argument between two of the kids downstairs in the family room.

I asked Isaac, "Should we let them battle it out, or should I go downstairs and try to mediate?"

"Take care of it," Isaac requested. "I have to get up in a few hours for work, and I need to sleep."

He was right. He had a much earlier morning than I did the next day. "Okay. I'm getting up."

The kids were fighting over control of the TV screen. (Sound familiar?)

The following drama played out.

Enter: Mom to break up the fight, quiet things down, and attempt to mediate.

The volume is now lower, but the temperature rises, with burning, hurtful words and heightened emotions as the sibling adversaries defend their positions.

Mom tries to give each an opportunity to speak. They keep interrupting and talking over each other, only seeing their side and not considering the other's point of view. It's late. Maybe best to pick this up after everyone has cooled down and is rested.

The TV screen is now turned off. The kids retreat to their rooms full of anger and resentment. To be continued. To be resolved—eventually. Until the next time.

End scene.

I'm figuring that this movie has played at everyone's house, more or less. Perhaps the personalities at your house are different, as are the temperaments, the ages, and the chemistries. And maybe your script and the atmosphere at your house are different too. But I'm guessing that the emotions and the harsh expressions, in whatever the chosen words, are the same. Yes? Yes.

And I suppose it should be expected. We teach our kids to operate with self-respect and confidence and to stand up for themselves and hold their ground when challenged in the outside world. We should expect them to do the same at home, and with even more steadfastness, because home is supposed to be their safe space, where they can be their 100% unfiltered selves, for better and for worse.

Sometimes the *worse* crosses lines, and that's when the hurricane hits. We, the parents, need to step in to set the record straight in the most rational, kind, and firm way, reinforcing the house rules and borders.

Yes, the opinions of our kids count, even when they are little, but so too do their siblings'. We need to remind them to be loving and patient with their siblings by explaining to them that each is at a different stage in life and that our approaches are colored by where we are on our journey. We may not agree, so we'll need to find a respectful way to agree to disagree and organize a plan that works for all.

There will be pushback, and it may not be a smooth conversation, but do your best to hold your ground and lead the conversation rather than let the conversation lead you.

How?

Once again, by defining your key messages and applying public relations and customer service practices at home.

That's a look at the picture from 500 feet above. Now let's zoom in a bit.

Zooming in

How do we stop our kids from engaging in combustive behavior? Scream? Physically intervene? Ignore? Quietly manage?

At work, I'd try to mediate if there was a team disagreement.

It all sounds so reasonable. Right? So why shouldn't it be the same at home when they start combusting in front of you?

Granted, when you are in the middle of something important, including and especially when trying to get a good night's sleep at the end of a long, hard day, it's so very hard to keep your cool and problem solve. Again, this is different than crisis management, where you really *need* to drop everything, focus, compartmentalize and deal with it.

Squabbles are not life-or-death, but they do seem to hit a really bad chord almost all of the time.

When I would be copywriting or editing and my kids would interrupt with loud fighting, my first thought was always: *SHUT the F up! Can't you see I'm working here?!?!*

Then, I'd try to mediate, sometimes after scraping them off each other. It was not always successful and not always done quietly. My bandwidth at that moment determined how gently or forcefully I spoke. I admit it. I've been known to roar.

And remember I told you I have made lots of mistakes? Managing emotions is the one I've messed up the most over the years at home. I know what I'm supposed to do, but execution, well, that's hit or miss.

My gut reaction is always to scream first. After all, I am a fiery Scorpio, born in the year of the dragon.

I am afraid that there have been many times when I have overreacted and that certain responses have been disproportionate to the offense. I'd raise my voice if they did something they clearly knew they shouldn't do, like lie, speak rudely, sass, or talk back. And I always hated it when my teens would accuse me of not helping them with something when I knew I did, or when they would instantly demand I find their missing shoes, coat, or notebook with two minutes to go before they would need to leave the house.

I never, however, got upset at mistakes, like when one of my kids would accidentally break something in the house or scratch the car while driving. In those cases, I might make a mention, but generally, I go quiet. Everyone makes mistakes. It's how we learn.

A Story

Isaac is the oldest of six children, the youngest one 20 years his junior, and from a half-Moroccan, half-Tunisian Jewish family. When "the baby" announced her engagement, we agreed to host a Henna, a Moroccan engagement party, at our house, complete with a full sit-down dinner in our garden, special Moroccan baked goods, Moroccan music, and the traditional dance ceremony where the women dress up in beautiful and colorful traditional Moroccan dresses called kaftans, and dance with trays of the Moroccan sweets in hand in front of the happy couple sitting on decorated chairs.

It was a big night.

Thirty-five guests arrived, the ladies changed into their Moroccan wear, and the living room was fully decorated in red and gold. A red carpet ran the length of the dining and living rooms, starting from the overflowing sweets table and ending at the other side of the room, in front of the bride's and groom's chairs, which were also fully adorned in red and gold.

One by one, the ladies danced up and down the red carpet to the beat of Eastern music with sweet trays stretched above their heads, as the men standing on both sides of the red-carpeted aisle clapped along. Eventually, all finally gathered with glee around the happy couple.

The Eastern music continued to boom.

Maya's phone—the source of the booming—was perched dangerously close to a large crystal bowl, which I was gifted long before I moved to Israel. Can you guess what's coming? With each beat, the bowl started to inch its way to the edge of the shelf of the breakfront where it had been placed. The vibrations continued until the crystal bowl finally slipped over the side of the shelf.

CRASH!

It smashed into smithereens on the cream-colored marble floor.

I wasn't in the room when it happened, but I heard it, along with my name being called loudly enough to hear over the noisy hum of the room and music. I walked over to see the damage, and everyone in the room looked at me, watching for my reaction.

Now, if this were you, what would you have done? Maybe on the inside, we freak out, just a little? I mean, I'd had that bowl for decades. Naturally, I was pissed. But then again, it was an accident.

I looked at the small crowd, including my slightly nervous daughter, and with a half giggle and smile, I said, "All good. It's not a party until something breaks."

The room exhaled, I swept up the crystal dust, and we continued to enjoy a glorious night.

While my insides may have instinctively boiled for a moment, I quickly understood that it was an unintentional mistake, and as the parent, I knew I needed to get a grip. And if you have even a little bit of a temper, you should get a grip as quickly as you can too. Mind over matter, my friend, whenever possible.

Finding Your Inner Charley

We all need to take a page from the book of my professional mentor, former boss, and friend, PR industry icon Charley Levine. He signed my *Ketubah*, my Jewish wedding contract, as a witness. That's how dear he was.

Charley was a very tall, brilliant, creative, and extraordinarily kind and friendly person. He was a presence when he walked into any room, worked with the top leadership in Israel and the United States, and BOY, could that man copy write, and FAST! Everyone loved and respected his opinion.

During the five years I worked with Charley, I NEVER saw him get upset about *anything*. I'd be so very concerned about something, and he'd talk me down every time. He took everything with a HUGE grain of salt.

Charley's lesson for all of us: *Don't take any of it to heart or let it bother you. Brush it off and move on to the next thing.* He did this so well!

As time rolled by, I got better at this lesson—not perfect, but better. I still raise my voice here and there, but not like I used to.

Managing emotions is not easy. In fact, it's hard. Sometimes we'll succeed, and other times not. If you fly off the handle for one thing or another, try to do better the next time. And I promise you, there will be a next time. There always is.

If you can, try to catch yourself in the middle of your tizzy and do a 180 redirect back to the land of self-control. You still get to be angry, just a controlled anger.

We have to remember that we are the adults here, and we need to keep it together, even when we feel like everything is disintegrating around us. YES! It's doable.

We do it with our colleagues, customers, and clients every day. We can do it with our kids at home. We all need to tap our inner Charley, me included. But how?

Let's break this down.

When we communicate, first we choose the message, then we choose our words and then we select the tone that both are delivered in.

You know the saying, *It's not what you say but how you say it?* *What* you say is your **message** and *how* you say it are the **words** and the **tone**.

When you speak to your clients and customers, **all three matter**. When you speak to your kids, all three matter even more.

Our kids internalize what we say in their inner core. What seems like a vanishing moment to us as parents, stays with our children, especially when the interaction was either heated or particularly gentle.

Let's put ourselves in our kids' shoes for a second. Have you ever been on the "other" side of public relations and customer service? Have you ever made a call asking for a company representative to help fix a problem?

How do you feel when you are *handled?* When they tell you nicely or otherwise to take a hike. When rather than helping you to fix your problem, they leave you no further along than you were before you called. Sometimes, it's not a big deal. But sometimes, this lack of help, delivered with a smile, is completely infuriating.

Once, I needed my passport number to be added to my negative PCR test results so I could fly back to Israel from the U.S. the next day. I was told the day before, prior to taking the test, that this could be done instantly after my test results were ready, likely within 24 hours. There was seemingly plenty of time. When I called the number I was given, the representative told me it would take another two days to process. I explained several times to this representative that another two days would be two days too late. The representative consulted with two of her managers who told her to tell me—nicely—they couldn't help. They were handling me, not helping me, and I was livid.

You can't PR a PR person, and I knew darn well this was doable. Plus, the price I would have to pay—more time away, money to change the date of my return flight, another PCR test somewhere else, and not being in the country when Maya had her first in-person army interview, and all because of their unwillingness to help—was unacceptable.

I doubled down.

It took a *keep trying* PR attitude on steroids (I nearly blew a fuse) and an understanding that I just needed to push long enough to find that one person willing to help. I was up against the clock. Luckily, I finally found someone on the pharmacy side who was willing to advocate for me with the people on the lab side. I promised her I would be as patient as she needed if she would help me. I waited for 35 minutes on hold, but this very kind woman, whose name I wish I could remember so that I could thank her here, found me a person on the lab side with the knowledge and willingness to help. Charming Ashley fixed my problem in literally five minutes.

From start to finish, the whole experience took a little more than two hours, but the urgency of the situation and the energy and pleading required made it feel like forever.

Helping, NOT Handling

Think that one experience was infuriating? This is how our kids feel every time they approach us to fix their problem and we blow them off. They grow frustrated, anxious, and more and more emotional, just like we do, attempt after attempt and going nowhere fast. They are asking to be helped, not handled.

When our kids interrupt us when we are working, for whatever the reason, perhaps they are not presenting their problem clearly and all we see are the temper tantrums and the sibling battles. But at the core of it, they are asking for help. If we want to be good *in-house* customer service and PR people, we need to find a way to help. Choose a message that includes a way to fix the problem, choose words that reflect the issue at hand, and choose a tone that is understanding and watch your child exhale.

There will also be times when you are interrupted by your kid doing something bad. In these cases, when delivering your message, try to choose words that separate the action from the kid. It's not a new strategy and certainly not something I created, but I find that using the "I-message" to deliver most messages during heated or serious discussions really works. We talked about this approach earlier too in Chapter 4, when we discussed one way to resolve sticky professional situations.

Now, let's apply it here. If your kids did something you considered bad, try addressing them this way:

"I really don't like **this**. **It** was really bad. And wherever the idea came from, understand that this is an example of what NOT to do. I know you are smart enough and talented enough to understand this and do better. Let's try not to revisit this again and go about it differently next time. How would you do it differently?"

Make sense? By not being accusatory and separating the person from the action, you have an opportunity to open a dialogue with your child. Delete the word "You" from the discussion when describing the event or how bad it was. When the situation is made abstract rather than personal, it's easier to accept the message of "Don't you dare do that again." Unless of course these very words are delivered with a smile and a hug and followed by an "I love you."

Sometimes the disturbances aren't heated at all. They are actually truly funny and border on the absurd. They may come at a very bad moment for you, but if you listen to the actual problem your kids are asking you to solve, it may induce a much-needed belly laugh.

"Mommy, who do you love the most?"

I was in the middle of copy editing. I thought, "Really? This now?"

With my face still staring at the computer screen, I answered the three of them standing behind me, "I love all of you equally."

They persisted.

"No, really, Mommy, who?"

I stopped what I was doing, turned to my children, looked them straight in the eyes and answered, with a full smile and a sarcastic tone, "Okay. I *hate* all of you equally."

They paused for a moment and then broke into laughter because they had also heard my father, their Pop Pop, answer this same question in this initially unexpected way. Pop Pop had delivered this response in the same sarcastic tone and smile on his face years earlier, and because the kids shared Pop Pop's sense of humor, they instantly knew that he was joking and burst into giggles. It was funny then. It was still funny during this exchange.

Years later, another absurdity, and this one truly hilarious, was the competition for the title of Best Omelet Maker.

Guy and Noa Lee were graciously making omelets for our family one evening as Isaac and I were working on some family business at the dining room table. Serves us right—of course there would be interruptions.

Our concentration was broken when Guy emphatically declared in a highly competitive tone, a sly smile on his lips and a sparkle in his eye, "Mine is better."

"No, mine is," insisted Noa Lee, equally lit up.

They looked at us, waiting for the verdict. "Well???"

I thought, *well, we were trying to do something here, but okay. Omelet competition it is.*

Isaac and I couldn't help but smile. It was funny, and the mood was light.

We tasted both omelets.

"They are both PERFECT—in different ways," Isaac and I agreed.

We all laughed. Yes, humor, validation, and balance go a long way.

Noa Lee and Guy are still both claiming the title of Best Omelet Maker.

Isaac and I are claiming that evening's public relations and customer service victories.

These types of victories can be yours too.

Put on your seatbelt and understand that you are in this for the long haul. Parenthood is a forever job. And no matter how old the kids get and *we* get, *they* are still the kids. The relationships may mature, but the personalities and the chemistry remain the same, more or less.

The next time you are interrupted by your child, take a quick moment to gain perspective, consider what they are really asking for, how you can help, and if now is indeed the time to help. Remember that they are persistent little PR people, just like at the agency, so you may need to redirect your attention away from work to achieve something equally productive. If that means giving your full attention to the kids and creating a nice memory, then so be it. Think in-house customer service and enjoy the break time.

Remember, when managing emotions:

- Take a quick moment to gain perspective
- Ask yourself: What are they really asking for? How can I help? Is now indeed the time to help?
- Remember your key messages and apply them to recurring issues
- Choose a mentor, like Charley, and ask yourself when things get tough or confusing: *What would they do?*
- Keep in mind: *It's not what you say but how you say it.* Message, words, and tone: All three matter!

- Watch your kids' reactions to your own reactions. Are your reactions helping or just handling?

If you would like to practice applying the public relations strategies above to your own story, please use your cell phone camera to scan the QR code below or use the hyperlink to access the free workbook that will walk you through the process. https://prfor.life/the-power-of-pr-parenting-login-page-qr/

CHAPTER 6

SAFETY AND TRANSPARENCY

(Note: This chapter includes references to violent sexual crimes that may be upsetting to some readers.)

In this chapter:

- Paying attention to both the big picture and the small details to keep your kids safe
- Preparing for the worst
- Coming back to those key messages
- Using client-preparation tactics to address the scary and unexpected

*If you see a knapsack on the ground without an owner, **DO NOT TOUCH IT!** Rather walk the other direction and call the bomb squad.*

This is one of several safety rules that I learned while working as the media liaison for the Israeli government in Boston, and which I still have a radar for in my daily life.

It taught me to try—emphasis on the word *try*, as I'm generally daydreaming about my action item list for the day—to scan an area with my eyes, take in a wide angle of what I am looking at, and simultaneously notice the little things along the way.

During my days in Boston, I lived on Charles Street in a second-floor apartment without an elevator. I came home from a social engagement one afternoon to find a package wrapped in brown paper at the bottom of the stairs just inside the building's entrance. Even in my usual daydream state, I couldn't miss it. I couldn't tell if it was addressed to anyone without touching it; there was no owner in sight and no visual signs that it had been delivered by the U.S. Postal Service or any other proper delivery service.

I instantly turned around, exited the building, and called the bomb squad. The one-man team arrived on the scene within minutes and investigated as required. False alarm. The package was harmless—just a short stack of books. I felt silly having called the bomb squad. The very nice police officer, wearing a protective vest, told me that it was okay, that they prefer endings like this, and that I had done the right thing, as you just never know. Better safe than sorry.

As parents, we need to try to always look at the big picture as well as notice the little things along the way in order to keep our kids safe. There are so many dangers lurking in and outside the house that could hurt the kids that sometimes it can be suffocating to think about it. In the old days, our focus was mainly on threats like drugs and alcohol, kidnappings, and physical and emotional attacks by mean boys or girls or unbalanced adults.

Today's world is even more complicated with school shootings, which have devastatingly become commonplace, highly-sexual and violent content on TV, the internet, and social media, as well as online bullying, which has graduated to a whole new level of torment. Whether the brutalizing is active or passive, heavy or light, it all hurts and can potentially lead to the unthinkable.

Instinctively, we want to keep our children safe by shielding them from every danger. Practically though, this is impossible. So, what do we do about it? We prepare them.

I used PR practices to do this.

For example, public relations professionals regularly prepare clients in advance regarding what to expect in an interview during a media training. We help them to fine-tune their key messages, practice delivering them clearly, succinctly, and colorfully, and coach them on how to answer tough questions.

We ask ourselves: *Is the prep sheet comprehensive, and has it been proofread? Did you double-check the client's wardrobe, hair, makeup, visual background, and quality of sound for their TV interview?* Miss one tiny but important detail and heaven help us. A prized opportunity is lost, or worse, there's a professional catastrophe.

We also know all of the interview parameters: time, location, length of interview, name and background of the interviewer, and the content interests. The more we know, the more we can help both our client and the journalist, and the better the end product. That's right, the more we know, the more we can help. The more the client knows, the better the interview.

Now let's apply this approach to parenting.

Doesn't it make sense to brief your children in advance on what to expect in school, on the playground, and online? And, doesn't it make sense to keep an eye on the *who, what, where, when, and why* of their movement, physical or virtual, and coach your child on what to say and how to handle possible scenarios, so if the time ever comes, they are ready for it?

What do I mean by this? Well, for example, we all know the "don't talk to strangers" rule. It's a standard rule, and yet it was the biggest challenge my mother had with me when I was a little one. I'd walk up to perfect strangers, just about anywhere, and with a big smile and lots of energy, say, "Hi, my name is Marjie. What's yours?"

Now granted, that natural behavior has been one of the keys to my success in PR, but back when I was a cute kid with short, light socket-tight curls, just like the child actress Shirley Temple, and a happy expression, this behavior was either a big hit at some family party or overwhelmingly alarming when in the presence of strangers.

Once I became a parent, the news reports of child abductions worldwide, and especially the disappearance of three-year-old Maddie McCann from her hotel room in Portugal in May 2007, really freaked me out. My youngest was two at the time. I was afraid.

It's a reasonable fear. According to the Office of Juvenile Justice and Delinquency Prevention (OJJDP), "In 2021, there were 337,195 reports of missing persons, involving youth, entered into the Federal Bureau of Investigation's National Crime Information Center (NCIC)."[11] It has also been published by The High Court that in the EU, the reported number of missing children every year is 250,000, and that in the U.S., this number is around 460,000.[12] I don't know about you, but this leaves me petrified.

In my effort for my children not to become part of this statistic, I exercised the preparation procedures that I used at work, with the kids at home. Rather than media training, though, we had "travel training". Each time before the kids and I would fly to the United States to visit my family, we'd practice playing "Airport" by going to the mall. Baby Maya would sit, locked into the stroller, while Guy and Noa Lee would each keep one hand on the handle of the stroller, Guy on the left and Noa Lee on the right, or vice versa. I placed my hands on theirs. If I could "feel" them, I didn't have to look at them to know they were with me. I felt in control.

I also told my kids about the abduction numbers and to be aware of the strangers at the kid play centers and amusement parks that we went to when we vacationed in the U.S. They knew to scream loudly and run to me in the event of trouble. I was always close by. We had fun, but we were also vigilant.

When they got a little older and would venture out of the house alone, I'd ask where they were going, who they would be with, and what time to expect their return. They didn't like this, as they felt it was a violation of their privacy. I explained to them that there should always be one person who knows where you are and when you plan to return at all times, so if you are not back by a certain time, then this should be taken as a warning that something is wrong and to take action. That one person is me as long as they are living at home. Also, if there is an emergency and their phone is off, I know where to find them.

We also talked.

From the start, no subject was taboo in our house. Well, almost: I never discussed money because I didn't ever want them to worry about that—if there was a financial issue, it was on Isaac and me to fix. And if Isaac or I had an illness, we would wait until we had the full story before sharing with the kids so that we would have the answers to their questions and would save them from the roller coaster ride of diagnosis.

Aside from that, sex, drugs, rock n' roll—ask away. And when the kids did ask about the definition of profane words, puberty, intercourse, mind-altering substances, whatever, we spoke with them openly, without judgment. We tried our best to do so as factually, directly, specifically, and as respectfully as we could, very much appreciating their comfort level with asking us these questions in the first place.

If we could squeeze it in, we'd ask them why they were asking and where the thought originated. All of this gave us a peek into our child's psyche and at least a small idea of what they were going through at the time. A pulse check. Is everything okay? Is assistance needed? Or should we just stay out of it and let them work it out?

There were also occasions when I proactively brought up the topics of sex, drugs, and rock n' roll and volunteered my perspective and experiences, along with those of family and friends. I wanted them to be able to use these case studies to hopefully color their thinking and, with any luck, save them some heartache and physical self-torture, like the kind that comes from excessive drinking and the dreaded hangovers that follow.

I told them about the time I traveled to Russia during my sophomore year in university and ended up in the hospital in Yalta for a couple of days with alcohol poisoning after a night out at the clubs pounding shot after shot. I told my kids about how I downed my share of the *scorpion bowls* at a bar the night after my last final, first semester, senior year in university, and woke up the next morning with a hangover so bad it hurt to brush my hair. Until today, I have an aversion to hard liquor, and this is why.

In the interest of transparency, though, I let my kids *taste* whatever alcoholic beverage we or friends were drinking at a party or a restaurant. This way, they knew what it was early on and hopefully concluded that it tasted disgusting and that they weren't missing anything. Every once in a while, they might indulge in having their own experience, but generally speaking, my kids, like their mother—albeit later in life—were the designated drivers and the ones holding their friends' heads over the toilet.

Talking. Briefing. Preparing. Transparency. It's important.

Let's get into the big picture-small details discussion now. In my opinion, the safety of our children depends on this too. And just when you least expect it, expect it.

We had just hosted 30 children and immediate family for Noa Lee's 7th birthday. That year, the entertainment was two brothers, one an adult, the other a teen, dressed as clowns and performing a magic act. At the conclusion, they gave out cotton candy. Fun was had by all.

After the last guest left, I closed the gate to the entrance of our house and began cleaning the hurricane left behind. I started with the dishes.

After around five minutes, it occurred to me: it's too quiet in this house. I thought maybe the kids were upstairs opening presents.

I approached Isaac, who was surfing on the computer in my office. I sat on his lap and kissed him.

"I love you," I said.

"Love you too. Great party," he replied.

"Thanks. Are the kids upstairs?" I asked.

"The older two went with my brother to my parents," he replied.

"And the baby?" I asked.

"I thought she was with you," he said with concerned surprise.

"I thought she was with you or the kids. Plus, the gate to the street is closed and she can't open it," I replied with growing fear.

I thought to myself: *Right. The heavy iron gate was closed. Where could she be?*

I jumped off Isaac's lap and ran upstairs to check the kids' bedrooms. No one.

I screamed my baby's name full blast. "MAYA!!!!" No reply.

"Call your brother to see if he has her," I yelled out to my husband. No. Maya wasn't with him.

We ran to the front garden. Holy crap. The gate was open. OMG! SHE OPENED THE GATE!!!!!

I told my husband to stay at home in case our two-year-old turned up, and I'd go out to look for her.

Where to start? One side of our quiet side street hugs a nature reserve and the other leads to a major street in the neighborhood with lots of cars. Both possibilities were terrifying.

I was running down our street as fast as I could, which frankly isn't exactly fast, deciding whether to continue right or left. The look of sheer terror on my face stopped a neighbor and his wife as they were turning onto our street in their vehicle on their way home.

"Everything okay?" they asked.

Already out of breath, I replied, "My little girl is missing."

"Oh, we just saw a little girl on the sidewalk of the main street. Some lady found her wandering. That must be her," said the husband of the couple.

Clearly understanding that he runs WAYYYY faster than me, he jumped out of his car and ran like the wind to tell the lady who found my baby that the mother was on the way and not to bother calling the police.

To this day, we call this neighbor The Man Who Saved Our Daughter.

By the time I arrived about a minute or so later, a small crowd had already gathered around the "lost girl".

To say I was relieved would be an understatement. I held my baby closely and thanked the lady for shielding her from harm. The crowd was first supportive, offering me water, which I respectfully declined.

With all in order, the crowd dispersed, now with the expression of judgment on their faces. How could this horrible mother have lost a toddler to wander onto a busy street?

Well, this horrible mother hadn't given her two-year-old enough credit for her quickly developing motor skills—a very important detail to notice.

When I returned to our house with Maya on my hip, I looked at Isaac, both of us still pumped with adrenaline. "I guess she knows how to open the gate handle. From now on, we should lock it," I declared emphatically.

My husband looked at me with an aggravated expression that can only be described as the visual translation of "Duhhhhh."

This experience was a red flag for me. Never underestimate your children at ANY stage. You'll be surprised at how quickly they grow and adapt and how clever they can be when it comes to problem-solving, like how to turn the handle of a heavy iron gate or pull over a chair to step on to reach a high light switch, like Guy did when he was a little boy.

When you do lock a gate or a door or adjust something else to protect them, like covering electricity outlets, softening the points of the coffee table, or electrically locking the controls of the stove, explain to them why you are doing this and discuss it to make sure that they understand the dangers of the alternative. If they understand, there's a fighting chance that they'll actually listen.

How do you know they understand? Just like in a media training regarding parameters and protocol, ask them to play it back by explaining to you what you just explained to them.

Maya had no idea that she was in danger when she left for her little adventure. She got a gentle earful though that evening; she played it back to me, even though she was two. Between that and the locking of the gate for a short time after to reinforce the message, we didn't revisit this situation again.

We need to remember that what's obvious to us isn't necessarily to our kids, at any stage. There's a first time for everything, and if we can, we need to prepare them for each leg of their journey to the best of our ability.

Crafting *Your* Key Messages

In PR, every new assignment begins with defining the client's target audience and crafting the key messages for each. From there, we build working scenarios, so that no matter the situation the client encounters representing the company, they know how to respond. There may be twists, turns, and the unexpected, but if they have been prepped, there is a better chance that they'll be able to handle the unexpected, as they keep in mind the lessons they've learned from their training and the key messages that they've rehearsed. Like with presentations, ONLY the message needs to be memorized, NOT the word choice or its order.

This PR practice can also be useful at home to prepare our kids, keeping in mind that target audiences—those our kids may encounter—and the key messages for each, are not-one-size-fits-all. Mine were crafted based on our particular situation: living in Israel and the United States. YOUR key messages would be based on what you know to be true in your life. Only YOU know your exact target audiences and what the appropriate key messages and responses would be in any given scenario. And although some messages might be universal, the way they are delivered may need to be tweaked for local flavor.

A PR example: When you issue a press release in multiple languages, the translations must keep in mind local nuances. What might sound good in English doesn't necessarily play well in Italian, Hebrew, or Japanese. So, adjustments are made to share the message in the way it will be most positively received in each location.

Same difference for our personal lives. We each have our own vantages.

With this in mind, I'd like you to pretend you are prepping for a TV or newspaper article interview. The topic is how to prepare your kids for stranger danger, bullying, and possible violent attacks like shootings. Below are the reporter's anticipated questions.

Now, even though you may have the anticipated questions in advance, you also need to be prepared for the follow-up questions. Remember those twists, turns, and the unexpected? As you prep, try to stay one step ahead.

Now give this a good think and tell me, based on what you know to be true, how would you advise your child to answer each of the questions below?

Please answer these questions in writing. And feel free to add as many questions to this list as you wish.

After you have answered these questions, put them away and come back to them a few days later and read back your answers. Make any edits you'd like and share with someone you trust to be your second pair of eyes for ideas and feedback.

Ready? Begin.

1. What should you do if a stranger offers you candy? One step ahead: What should you do if that stranger tells you they're selling it to benefit your school/sports team/etc.?
2. What should you do if someone you don't know tells you to get into their car? One step ahead: What if the person tells you convincingly that Mommy or Daddy was delayed or hurt?
3. What should you do if an adult or another child tries to touch you or manages to touch you in your private spots or if they ask you to touch them in their private spots? One step ahead: What if they threaten you or someone you love in any way, physically or emotionally, if you tell?
4. What should you do if kids are being mean or threatening? In-person or online? One step ahead: What if they are physically violent in person or frightfully aggressive online?
5. What should you do if you hear gunshots? One step ahead: What if the gunman is outside or in front of your classroom?

If you have completed the exercise above, you now have at least some of the important key messages that you can share with your child to help equip them to deal with trouble. The next step is inviting them for a heart-to-heart talk to share your key messages, define for whom each is intended, and then practice them together.

Of the five questions above, we practically dealt with two: bullying and sexual predators. Let's start with bullying, which was a recurring theme, not only by other kids, but also by certain teachers. Yes, the teachers, which can come in a variety of forms—a classroom teacher, a coach, or an after-school activity instructor. The short of it is: Adults in positions of authority have been known to bully kids.

Regarding the bullying by the other kids, in most cases, I stayed out of the drama, knowing that one day kids are fighting and the next day, they are friends again. Best for them to work it out themselves.

In PR, sometimes listening, smiling, and being seemingly agreeable is the best way to avoid or defuse useless conflict. I'm not a *yes* person when asked my opinion or when it comes to advising my clients, but sometimes, when a client is clearly upset with something, the best course is to listen, empathize, acknowledge their feelings, and move on to the next thing with lessons learned. Translation to parenting—as my maternal grandfather used to say, and I'm paraphrasing now—*if ultimately it won't hurt anyone, and it truly won't change anything, other than make the other person feel good, let the other person be right, even if they're wrong and move on from it.*

If the bullying graduated to something physical, however, which is crossing a line in my book, I would call the other parent(s) and a teacher, if relevant, talk it out and hopefully, at the end of the discussion, all the *adults,* at least, were on the same page with a common goal and action items to achieve this goal. Sometimes, it worked. Sometimes, it didn't. Parents never want to hear that their child was aggressive or violent. And sometimes, certain parents never spoke to me again. How dare I accuse their child? Even so, they heard it and were aware, even if they were in denial, at least publicly.

That said, at no time did I social engineer. I never told my child not to play with another, even if I wasn't fond of the kid or the other kid's parents. I would never tell a colleague or a client not to work with someone they were considering, even if I wasn't a fan. I wouldn't do it to a colleague and certainly not to a kid. Their choices are their own. And to do anything other than that is no more than reverse bullying. Again, in all likelihood, today's bully could be tomorrow's best friend. It was always interesting to see how the dust settled after any given drama.

Now, let's discuss the teachers. I have the greatest respect for teachers. My mother was a teacher. My niece is studying to become a teacher and some of my favorite people in the world are educators. It's a very difficult job to teach and control a classroom full of young people. I'm sure that I couldn't do it. It's also an enormous responsibility knowing you are molding the minds of the future. There are some brilliant educators out there who have made a truly positive impact on the lives of their students. Unfortunately, the opposite is also true.

Of all the bullying my kids experienced, the passive-aggressive behavior of some of the classroom teachers over the years was the most challenging and upsetting. In most cases, we let things slide rather than take action. Like in PR, sometimes it's best just to keep your mouth shut with a difficult client. No sense in arguing. Get the job done, complete the project, and move on. Same with the teachers that bullied. We advised our kids that sometimes the best key message is silence and the best plan is to do nothing other than to keep those eyes on the academic donut and score really well.

I'd tell them, "Water off a duck's back." And I'm paraphrasing again now: *Whatever mean thing the teacher said to you in front of the entire class or did to try to break your concentration during a test, let it go, try to regain your focus, and get the work done. If the teacher is short with you, avoids you or your questions, or gives you a mean look, try not to take it personally or to heart. This situation is not permanent. This year will end. Hopefully, you will have learned something from this teacher, and then it will be time to move on.*

However, if your child's personal well-being is being threatened, then you must take action. For two years, a couple of Maya's teachers had crossed a line, slowly and passive-aggressively, to an eventual point where the learning environment was so toxic that Maya's emotional and physical well-being had deteriorated. There was one teacher who, in my experience and opinion, was so cruel and unbalanced, that I knew in advance not to even bother approaching her because nothing good could come from it, no matter how PR friendly I was.

The straw that broke the camel's back came during a parent-teacher meeting. Maya literally left the room to vomit, she was so intimidated. The teacher, who had always been so friendly and spot-on professional with me, sat behind her desk, unmoved and icy.

I understood then what my child had been trying to tell me all along—that some teachers have one set of behavior for the parents and another set for the students. In that moment, I decided that enough was enough. It was best to exit left. I pulled Maya out of this school and enrolled her at another one to start the following September. Maya was punished on her report card that year for missing class to attend the required tryouts for the other school. We didn't care. Bye Bye, Bullies!

Be it a class, a school club, or an out-of-school activity, the same applies. Assess the facts and determine what next move will be the healthiest for your child.

Sexual Harassment

As you and I both know very well, danger isn't limited to the school grounds. It also lurks on the way to and from, and especially on public transportation, which is a majorly fertile ground for trouble. This brings me to the second category we had to deal with in addition to the bullying.

Three times sexual perverts either assaulted or threatened my girls, who were minding their own business as they stood in the aisle on public transportation during daylight hours. They have also been harassed multiple times when they were simply walking down the street on their way to and from public transportation on the final leg to school or home.

Please don't ask what they were wearing. It is completely irrelevant. They could be wearing string bikinis or paper bags; such things should still NEVER happen.

In one case, my daughter told the perpetrator off in full volume on the bus before he could graduate his advances. In another case, my daughter called me straight away, so I could start problem-solving before she arrived home.

How did I feel? In all cases, heartbroken, frustrated, and angry. Heartbroken because some creepy stranger had hurt or tried to hurt my child, and my child was suffering from that trauma. Frustrated and angry because I wanted justice for my children, and the police, well-intentioned or not, were useless in helping us get it.

Now imagine you are looking at my face and into my eyes. Now imagine an expression with the greatest disgust and my eyes burning with fire and hear me: What is important to understand is that their experiences are not uncommon—not in Israel, not in the U.S., and not worldwide. No matter where you live, I'd bet you can find alarming data regarding harassment on public transportation.

I'll never forget reading the horrific news about Jyoti Singh, the 23-year-old physiotherapy intern who, even though she was accompanied by a male friend, was beaten, gang-raped, and tortured in a private bus in India by the other passengers and the bus driver and later died of her injuries.

I was shocked, angry, and afraid for all of our daughters taking public and private transportation. I wondered: *How do we protect our girls from such things?* Jyoti should have been safe on that bus. And yet she wasn't. I also thought about this young girl's family and the devastation they are suffering. A hurt never to be healed.

Here's one recent case study: An online survey conducted by Metro Magazine and published in May 2020 showed that *of the 891 students at San José State University polled, verbal harassment was the most common form of harassment, with 41% experiencing "obscene/harassing language" and 26% being subjected to sexual comments. Among non-verbal types of harassment, 22% had been stalked and 18% had been victims of indecent exposure. Physical harassment was less common, but still 11% of students had experienced groping or inappropriate touching.*[13]

The article goes into detail regarding the types of sexual harassment experienced, including *how transit riders, and especially women, are often victims of a wide range of offenses of a sexual nature that happen on buses and trains, as well as at bus stops and train stations.*[14]

You may be thinking: This is one campus, one hyper-localized problem, but the polls show again and again that it's a refrain heard on a global level.

From our experience and from speaking with others, we know it can happen so quickly, like a hit and run, that by the time you are aware of what just occurred, the offender is long gone. It also happens in crowds, and generally goes unseen by others, and happens out of the frame of the limited number of security cameras on the bus or train.

And though riding during daylight hours can help, it's not foolproof. Daylight did not protect my children.

This brings us back, once again, to defining the target audience and key messages. This is a practice I revisit regularly with my clients, generally every three months or sooner, depending on the pace of progress, and always to reflect the current reality and goals of the company.

Ready? How would you want your child to answer these questions?

1. What do you do if you are standing or sitting on public transportation next to someone who makes you feel uncomfortable for any reason?
2. How can you prove that someone attacked you?
3. How can you get a hold of evidence held by the city or state?
4. If you are attacked, whom should you tell?
5. Should you file a police report?
6. How should you act or react when approached or assaulted?
7. Should you try to take pictures or video?
8. How should you handle the post-trauma of the attack?
9. Is therapy a good idea?
10. What should you NEVER do during or after an attack?

Add to this list of questions as you wish. And again, write your answers down, read them back again in a few days, and have someone you trust take a look to offer feedback. Make your changes understanding that the point of these key messages is to empower your child according to what you feel is the right thing to do, while safeguarding their emotional and physical well-being. Most importantly, it's for both of you to know what to do if ever tested.

Cyber Dangers

We've talked about ground attacks. Now let's take a look at those launched online, actively as well as passively.

Kids are navigating the full gamut of online communication—from their friends, family, creeps, and snarky businesses alike. This is why I encourage my kids to let me know what forums they are joining. I remind them that online people aren't always what or who they say they are, and that they don't have to be friends with everyone. They can block them, and if something really seems odd, they should show it to me.

If necessary, I'll answer on their behalf, like when Maya was approached by a sports apparel company to be an influencer, even though her social media following is purposely limited. That was an alarm for me, especially having been part of a reputable marketing team that considered hiring known teen influencers to promote consumer products. I discussed and agreed with Maya what to text back to this company before blocking them.

The mean-girl and mean-boy syndrome and the drama it produces are at a crescendo with social media. It's not enough to have to deal with supposed friends running hot and cold on you at school or at activities—one day nice, the next day not. In the old days, you could get a break after you went home. Not today. The communication is 24/7.

Today, it's easy to see who is doing what at any moment of the day. The kids are regularly posting *everything*: what they are eating and wearing as well as who they are partying with, which also tells you who they didn't invite to the party.

My children constantly remind me that today's world is different from when I grew up and that I just don't understand. Maybe. But the way I see it, bullying is bullying, no matter how it is packaged or on what platform it is exercised. And you and I very well know, as parents, it's very difficult to see your child upset and obsessing over the dreadful actions or painful words of another kid or group of kids.

I would say to my kids during one of these dramas, "We are not going to give this kid the power to determine if our day today will be good or bad. Let's take back control."

We take control by filling our children with self-confidence and self-respect and strongly advising them to adopt an approach to ONLY fill their lives with people who bring them sunshine, and ONLY sunshine. If they can't avoid someone who they consider toxic, perhaps recommend that they pull out those imaginary earplugs that we talked about earlier to try to filter out the meanness and not to take the negativity to heart.

I have always encouraged my kids to behave nicely and politely, to be a lady or a gentleman, but not to marshmallow in the face of nastiness, and if there is an injustice, to respectfully stand their ground. I urge them not to wait until they turn 50 to adopt this philosophy.

I think the best way to teach our children to stand tall is to help lift them into the sunshine. How? Constantly remind them of their enormous value, shower them in love, and listen, even when they think you aren't.

To borrow my favorite line from the movie *The Help*, I regularly remind my children that they are smart, kind, and important. I also add special and beautiful to the list, because this is also how I see them and how I'm sure you see yours too. I tell them over and over again, to reinforce it and with the hope that with enough repetition, it will finally sink in, and they will believe it too. We believe the bad stuff when we hear it enough. It should be the same with the good stuff. And hearing the good stuff never gets tiring.

During the discussion following any given high drama, I'll hug them, tell them I love them, and make a joke or do an impression related to the conversation to make them laugh. Laughter always helps. Throughout, I listen, as much as my attention span will let me. If I need a short break, I excuse myself to go to the bathroom or get a drink and then return to listening.

On a daily basis, like at work following a client interview or an event, we debrief the morning after a party or school event. If they are tired or in a rush, then we debrief in the evening. We discuss the good, like a compliment that made them feel good, as well as the bad, perhaps some upsetting interaction with a friend or a disappointment discovered on social media. And, of course, any bullying going on.

Again, I hug them and remind them just how amazing I think they are. I repeat for the millionth time that I love them and am proud of them. You can never say that enough. I remind them of their positives at every opportunity, hoping the good replaces whatever poor or questionable self-esteem that may still remain in their psyche.

If we are in public, I have been known to whisper such affirmations in their ear, hoping they will eventually hear my voice in their subconscious, like Jiminy Cricket from the Disney movie, *Pinocchio*, especially at a difficult crossroads.

Often, my help is unwanted. In frustration, occasionally, my kids nicely accuse me of ignorance. "You know nothing, Mom! Leave me alone." Sound familiar, Jon Snow? Exhausting! Right?

But we keep trying because, just like in PR, where we need to help our clients achieve their goals, it is our job as parents to help our kids achieve theirs.

Remember:

- Open communication is only step one
- Key messages are the bridge between how you want your kid to react in a crisis and their ability to remember under duress
- Key messages should mature with your child, as new experiences require new vigilance
- Practice what-if scenarios
- Positive reinforcement is the ultimate confidence-builder

If you would like to practice applying the public relations strategies above to your own story, please use your cell phone camera to scan the QR code below or use the hyperlink to access the free workbook that will walk you through the process.

https://prfor.life/the-power-of-pr-parenting-login-page-qr/

CHAPTER 7

BUILDING SELF-RELIANCE

In this chapter:

- Teaching persistence
- Overcoming separation anxiety
- Showing your kids how to believe in themselves and go for it
- Preparing the flight from the nest

In 1983, Michael Dukakis was re-elected Governor of Massachusetts. That same year, I was a freshman at Boston University with dreams of becoming a television journalist. I was young, ambitious, and eager to get an interview with the new governor and to publish a story in the Daily Free Press, Boston University's student newspaper.

I called the governor's press secretary requesting some time. No room. I started to call the press secretary weekly.

"Hi. It's Marjie. How are you? Any room in the calendar for me next week?"

"Fine. Thanks. Sorry. Still no room," she'd reply.

"Okay. Thank you."

After around three months of this, the press secretary, who by then knew my voice—mind you, this was before the days of caller ID and mobile phones—finally gave me my shot. She told me that I had been so nicely persistent that I had earned some time with the governor: 15 minutes. I was thrilled.

I borrowed a dress that could pass as professional from a friend in my dorm, and off I went, tape recorder and questions in hand, to interview the governor in his office at the Massachusetts State House in Boston. Governor Dukakis greeted me with a firm handshake and a warm smile and invited me to sit in one of two chairs placed opposite one another. I pushed record on my tape recorder to start the interview. No light. The tape recorder wasn't working. Yes, I had checked the batteries earlier in the day and that the tape recorder was working. I couldn't believe it.

I thought: *OH SHIT! Three months of preparation, and it comes down to this.*

With pleading eyes, I asked if I could have some time to fix it. The governor was very polite and patient, and rather than kick me out, he and I each fiddled with the tape recorder until *finally* it started working again. Exhale. But now I had *ten* minutes to interview the governor.

I remember the interview lasted less than that as he answered my two pages of questions thoroughly but succinctly. We took a picture together and shook hands again.

I thanked him, and just like that, my 15 minutes were up. I wrote a Q&A format article that made the front page of The Daily Free Press my freshman year. Score!

There are a few morals to this story. First, gentle, respectful, and kind persistence can pay off. Secondly, a *professional* "no" can possibly turn into a "maybe", and ultimately a "yes". Thirdly, be nice to everyone, no matter their rank. You never know who might write a book and tell a story about you someday.

Governor Dukakis was a gentleman, took me seriously even though I was an 18-year-old rookie, was patient, helped me out of a bind, and gave me a fantastic interview. Governor, if by some remote chance you are reading this, thank you.

Persistence Pays Off

Painstaking persistence, self-confidence, the ability to weather what feels like a never-ending stream of nos and hang-ups, and following through to the end are all prerequisites for success, no matter what you do, though I'd argue, especially so in international public relations. We run after reporters and producers day and night, depending on the time zone, and it's always a marathon, never a sprint, with the goal of being of service to both your client and the media with the same effort.

You can spin your wheels for months at a time getting nowhere. It's discouraging and frustrating. The radio silence from unanswered emails or texts is deafening, and while the nos are disappointing, at least you know then to move on.

There are also those times when, eventually, someone says yes, and THIS is what makes the rest of it worth it, like when the national TV show producers booked my client for a segment on their program that aired nine months after the first pitch email was sent. Nine months. NINE MONTHS! I could have had a baby in the same amount of time. Both my babies and the TV placement were worth the wait.

Speaking of babies, what do these stories have to do with parenting? Instilling a sense of confidence and drive in your children is crucial because, at some point, the time will come when they will leave the nest, and you want to know you did your best to enable them to fly.

We are nervous, excited, and heartbroken all at the same time the day they take their first steps out of the house on their own. What makes it easier though is knowing that you have equipped your children with the self-reliance, persistence, and fortitude to keep trying, knowing that they'll face uphill battles, and like in PR, a long series of NOs along the way.

How do we equip them for this uphill climb? Leading by example, sharing your personal stories, and continuously encouraging your kids, especially when they doubt their abilities, are afraid of rejection, or get discouraged from defeat.

Teaching Our Kids PR Persistence and Self-reliance: Rejection, Rejection, Score

I told my kids the story of finding my first job after earning my first university degree in broadcast journalism.

I applied for tons of jobs during the second semester of my senior year to be a TV reporter. I got so many rejection letters I could wallpaper my entire student apartment bedroom in Allston, Massachusetts with them. It got to the point where I compared rejection letters to see which TV station wrote the best one. It turned into a bit of a game, and I kept applying for jobs on autopilot.

Then one day, during a follow-up call for one of my job applications, a local TV news director of a mid-market station picked up the phone by some miracle and was actually nice. Usually, some random person would answer the phone and brush me off, or, if I did manage to get someone on the line with some power, they were usually short with me as well.

I must have caught this particular guy on a good day, because he took three minutes out of his very busy newsroom day to mentor the kid on the other end of the receiver. Again, this was 1986, still way before the smartphone was introduced.

He kindly explained, "Marjie, I have a stack of resumes on my desk from reporters with ten years of experience. This is what you are competing with."

I replied, "Only ten years, huh?" and started laughing. He laughed with me.

He understood that I had picked up on his hint and kindly suggested that I try a small, non-union TV station, and then recommended two. I followed his advice and landed a weekend anchor/weekday reporter job with one of them that started two weeks after I graduated college. I think I was one of three people in my graduating class at BU's College of Communication that year who landed an on-air TV job straight after graduation. Just like with the interview with Governor Dukakis, the persistence had paid off.

Setting a Good Example... And Knowing What You're in for

My kids had a front-row seat to my habit of not giving up unless I really had to give up, both personally and professionally. For example, I had to give up getting justice for my daughter after she was attacked on public transportation because we had no way to identify the attacker. But, if there's even the slightest ray of hope, I'm a little like a pit bull. I get an idea in my head, and I have a hard time letting go. I have to turn over every stone when trying to achieve a goal.

Though my pit-bullism drives Isaac nuts, it has rubbed off on our kids in a positive way. They execute the same, in their own style and oftentimes in a gentler way, like when Maya turned 16 and decided she wanted to get a job and earn her *own* money.

On her own initiative, she went from store to store at several malls in our area, checking who was hiring and interviewing. She also monitored her social channels for help-wanted posts. This went on for months. She got a lot of nos because she wasn't 18 or 21 years of age, or they didn't need more workers. Eventually, after pounding the pavement for a while, she finally found work, first at a local wedding catering service, then at an amusement park, and later at a neighborhood ice cream parlor. Score!

Pit-bullism can also backfire when the kids get it into their heads that they want something you decide to veto. Whether you have a toddler, teen, or young adult, I think we have all experienced backtalk, sass, and rudeness, as they attempt to test our boundaries and see how far they can push us. When they are little, they may not want to go to sleep at bedtime, or to do their homework, or share a toy or their sweets. When they get older, they may want to take the car to drive hours away to visit a friend, stay out late on a school night, or stay out *all* night at a weekend party.

"Explain to me why. I want to understand your reasoning why you are saying no," mine would insist, sometimes so loudly, I'm certain the neighbors could hear.

"I don't owe you a reason. The answer is no," either Isaac or I would reply, first emotionless and later more firmly, as they would continue to lobby.

They hated this answer and told me years later it would only encourage them to lie and do what they wanted anyway. In retrospect, if we had come up with a reasonable and rational argument at the top of the discussion, *why* we were saying no, perhaps we could have preempted the argument.

But sometimes, you just want to say "no" and not have to explain yourself to a teenager, and on these occasions, we'd go in circles. We'd do our best to hold our ground and keep our cool, which wasn't always the case. They'd stomp off and slam their door shut and return minutes later to try again, this time with even more gusto.

Exhausting. It would have been easier to say "yes", and sometimes, their stamina would outlast ours, or they'd make such a reasonable and rational argument that we'd cave. On the really important things, though, like when it influenced safety or health, we'd dig our heels in and not relent, no matter how high the drama. So, case by case.

Seeing Past the Frustrations

The bad news: This behavior is oftentimes considered very, very rude.

The good news: This behavior showed full self-confidence, a strong belief in their mission, and fabulous lobbying skills, no matter how frivolous we thought their request was. Naturally, we'd ask questions along the way to gain information, but also for them to practice clearly articulating their position, and if the opportunity presented itself, improve their English (yup, that again)—the silver lining to any fight or disagreement with the kids.

Now, whether you have a pit-bull personality or not makes no difference. You do whatever makes sense and feels comfortable for you. I think what does make a difference, though, is to begin honing self-confidence and persistence in our kids very early on, *and especially,* if you are a working parent, during the daycare years.

This is a very difficult time for all working parents *and* for our children, who are used to the comfort and stability of always having mom or dad around.

Maternity leave in the U.S. can be up to 12 weeks, none of which is guaranteed to be paid. I was lucky to stretch it to six months—three months paid, three months not—for each birth. But then, it was time to go back to work to help support our family. Israel is an expensive place to live. As of the day of this writing, the *cost of living* here, on average, is 8% higher than in the U.S.[15] Regardless, I think we can all agree that, for many of us, the extra salary really makes a difference.

So, I *had to*, but I also knew, that for me, going back to work was a healthy choice. I wanted to continue pursuing my career goals in tandem with being a mom.

It was also time for my babies to start expanding their universe beyond the confines of our home and wherever the wind blew us with that day's set of errands, like the grocery store, a doctor's visit, or a social engagement with a friend.

It was with a heavy heart that I dropped off Guy, my first baby, that first day at a daycare, 15 minutes from our tiny, three-room apartment at the time. We chose this daycare because of its fine reputation. The kids took nature walks on the property to see animals like cows, chickens, dogs, cats, etc., and enjoyed home-cooked meals and snacks. There was a great child-to-caregiver ratio, with a staff of three to four helpers led by a registered nurse.

The registered nurse ran a tight ship, with a huge smile, loads of encouragement, years of excellent experience, and a kindness that put both parent and child at ease. Guy and I were both in good hands, which was especially important that first year as Isaac was working abroad for the next six months then, which meant I was doing the single-working-mom thing.

This was the time period when, morning person or not, I was up in the middle of the night if Guy needed something, then up again early in the morning to organize my baby and pull myself together, drop off Guy, work a ¾ day following an hour commute with traffic to the office, do the mom thing in the latter part of the afternoon/early evening with playdates, meal time, bath and bedtime, and then finish off work stuff before watching whatever mindless TV show I was into at the time before passing out. Am I playing your song?

It was a tough time, but Guy was a relaxed and easy-tempered baby, and the policy was to ease the kids into daycare with the parent staying with their baby the first three days for up to a half day, though less and less each day.

Departures were tough, no matter what. Guy cried and pleaded for me to stay. And oh, did my heart sink. The separation anxiety was unbearable.

But the registered nurse gently urged me out the door. She picked up Guy and held him lovingly. We both told him I'd return in a few hours. I kissed Guy, wished him a great day and lots of fun, and swiftly exited.

I was out of sight now, but not out of earshot. I wanted to know for sure that everything was okay. So just like I would during an in-studio, TV interview for my clients, I found a way to eavesdrop, out of sight. I'd stand just outside of the doorway and listen to hear if what the registered nurse had promised me would be fulfilled—that after a matter of minutes, Guy would settle down and redirect into the morning's activity.

Yes, she was right. When I *heard* all was in order, I left, heart still wrenching, but satisfied that my child had begun a healthy journey outside of the house, was learning to socialize, and would benefit from all of the educational and motor skill enrichment that the daycare offered at the time. Remember, this was a Hebrew-only speaking daycare and another step forward for my child to becoming multilingual and multiliterate.

Trial and Error

I think it's important to encourage our kids to try their hand at whatever comes their way, has caught their attention, and what you might consider a necessity. In our house, "must-haves" were learning how to swim, some version of music instruction, and some level of observation of all the Jewish holidays for a sense of tradition and community belonging.

As you may recall from earlier chapters, nothing had to be done perfectly, and it was about the fun and the experience. However, if they DID show some special talent for something—music, art, sports, whatever—we encouraged them to take it as far as they could go. It didn't matter if they succeeded or not, though they had enough successes along the way to strengthen their sense of self and enough failures to know that it doesn't always work out, and that's okay too.

From this approach, all three have grown to adopt a strong work ethic. There were times when they started behind the 8-ball for one reason or another, but then would rise to the occasion to triumph, including with academic pursuits.

Guy wanted to go to a top university to study computer science and statistics. His high school grades were very good, but they needed to be even higher for what he wanted to study after the army. What's great about Israel is that you get as many do-overs as you want to bring up your high school average and your college entrance test scores. Another route is to enroll in a college preparation program, which is called and pronounced in Hebrew *mih-hee-nah*, and to make the necessary grades to be accepted into a university program.

Guy opted to go to *mih-hee-nah*. He studied diligently, stayed the course, partied very little, if at all during this time, and crossed the finish line at the end of the academic year. He had earned the super high grades required and was accepted into the coveted university computer science and statistics program of his choice.

In junior high school, Noa Lee wanted to be in the *Excellent* science class. There were two ways to be accepted: score high on the entry test for the class or get 100 in the regular class and bump up. She didn't score high enough on the entrance test, so she was going to have to work for it. Noa Lee wasn't deterred. She consistently scored 100s on her tests and projects in science class. After each 100, she'd ask her teacher if she could move up. The answer was always no. She continued to achieve 100s throughout the year. And, alas, at the end of the year, her science teacher still wouldn't approve her promotion. Noa Lee was very frustrated. She asked me to help. I went to the school and spoke with the assistant principal, who reviewed Noa Lee's grades, secured a confirmation of achievement from her head teacher, and declared: *Noa Lee has earned it. If she wants to go to this class, she's in.*

Noa Lee was thrilled, as in addition to the extra hours of science class which she loved, it meant participating in field trips to the prestigious Weizmann Institute of Science in Rehovot. Her persistence and hard work had paid off, as had Guy's.

Now the point here isn't how smart my kids are, but the effort that was made and the persistence in which it was carried out.

There are lots of smart people. What makes the difference is whether they have the confidence and willingness to try and try again, *and* even if just for the experience, if it comes down to that. *Better to try and fail, than not to try at all.*

Show up, learn what you can—academic or otherwise—participate and keep with it. Even when it feels like you're climbing the steepest mountain, you will always come away with something in your hand. And to me, that means you are a winner.

How to convince our kids of this?

In public relations, when we debrief with a client following an interview or presentation, we first review the successes and then note the things to adjust for the next time. In all cases, the message is delivered in the affirmative as we try to inspire our client to keep climbing that mountain. The same should go for our kids, right?

Continuously cheer the kids on—win, lose, or draw—and let them know emphatically that they are unconditionally loved and appreciated (you are always a star in my book) and that if they put their minds to it, they can accomplish whatever they set out to do with persistence, hard work, and follow through. And if for some reason it doesn't work out, all good. There's always a plan B. In fact, there are 26 letters in the alphabet, so there are at least 26 ways to try to achieve any goal.

It may not be an easy road. There will be lots of nos, disappointments, and naysayers along the way. But you and I need to keep injecting positive energy into our kids and inspire them to go the distance. If they win, well, it's a happy day. If they don't, no big deal, it's STILL all good, and the effort was worth it.

If our kids have a strong sense of security, feel loved, and know, without a doubt, where their next meal is coming from, and that you, their parent, will return at the end of the day, and that if real trouble comes, we are only a phone call or a text away—they can exhale and get on with it, whatever the day brings, throughout their lives and, as early as that first full week at daycare.

The separation anxiety in those first days, once crippling for both parent and child, slowly and almost completely disappears as time goes by. You still miss them and pang at departure, but it's not as dramatic as in the beginning. Drop off becomes swift, the kids wave goodbye and, within seconds, are already on to the next thing, just like Guy and Noa Lee at the registered nurse's baby house. (Maya went elsewhere—but that's another story.)

Now, blink your eyes. Our little ones are no longer babies. We may look at them and still see our babies, but the reality is they are budding adults striking independence.

Striking Independence

Ahhh, the teen years. This is the stage that can best be described by my favorite snippet from a verse written by lyricist Edward Kleban for the Broadway musical *A Chorus Line*. It goes like this: "Too young to take over. Too old to ignore. Gee, I'm almost ready. But. What. For?"

Since all of my kids began their teen years, they wanted independence. This included taking the bus to get around (rather than me driving them) and enjoying outings with their friends. I had a problem with this, mainly because a bus that I had taken regularly when I first moved to Israel had exploded on February 25, 1996, in a terrorist attack that killed 17 civilians and nine soldiers.

I could easily have been on that bus that day, and that event was my motivator to buy my first car in Israel. It also took me two decades to get back on one of those things, and at that, for a very short ride.

During their teen years, my kids were respectful but annoyed with me. All of their friends were taking the bus to Jerusalem, Tel Aviv, and the beach. I was very hesitant, bordering on paranoid, to let them ride the bus, to a point where Guy missed out on joining a popular social group, a 30 to 45-minute bus ride from our house, and Noa Lee missed out on various outings with her friends. My fear got in the way, and the separation anxiety was too much for me. Eventually, however, I had to get over myself.

Yes, as parents, we all need to get a grip and understand that the teen years mean giving our kids our blessing to fly free and grow, like when we let Noa Lee travel to Spain the summer before her senior year and when we let Guy fly across the world to join a backpacking teen tour in Alaska the summer before *his* senior year in high school. We hugged them, waved goodbye, and wished them the best of luck for a grand adventure. I cried like a baby on the car ride home from the airport. They, on the other hand, couldn't wait to get on the airplane.

That's the way it should be. They are out there, doing their thing and living their best lives. Sad that our job as parents feels nearly done (emphasis on the nearly). Nearly, because deep in our hearts, we know that parenthood is a lifetime job. And we can be sure that our children remember what we said repeatedly, just like we remember the wisdom or otherwise from our elders or professional mentors.

Whenever debating what might be the best choice for me, I hear my paternal Grandma say: *Always respect yourself.* Throughout the twists and turns of my career, I would hear my maternal and paternal grandfathers encourage: *Learn a skill and open up your own business.* I eventually did. And before I put my signature on any document, I ALWAYS hear my maternal grandmother warn: *You better read it before you sign it.*

I remember the humor and the family-first motto of my father. I hear my mother reminding me *there isn't anything you can't do if you try* and urging me to fix my hair. (She never likes my hair!) And professionally, whenever I am questioning myself, I hear my mentor Charley say: *You've got this.*

I'm sure you hear your parents, grandparents, and mentors when you are at your various crossroads throughout the day, be it choosing what to wear, what to eat, or how to handle someone or something at work or with the kids. What pops into your head during these times? What has stuck with you?

Indeed, these memories have stuck with both of us.

I wondered, though, what have we said that has stuck with our kids?

So, as I was writing this book, without warning, I asked my kids, "When you think of me or are not sure what to do about something, do you hear me in the back of your head, and if so, what am I saying? First thought!"

> Guy: "Eye on the donut." (There's Aunt Nancy again!)

> Noa Lee: "Your opinion counts (that's mine), and you can do anything." (There's my mother.)

> Maya: "When someone is being mean, water off a duck's back." And "If someone comes up to you and tells you that they are mommy's friend and that you sent them to take me—run away. Mommy has no friends! Stranger danger!" (Those two are mine too.)

Now I have a question for you. If you asked your children this same question, what do you think they'd say? What would you want them to say? And why? When they get home from school today, ask them.

By equipping our children with self-reliance, confidence, and drive, little by little, we actually manage to strengthen the bond with our children that, perhaps, will also stretch to future generations.

It was my parents and grandparents that I heard in the back of my head as I was pursuing that interview with Governor Dukakis. It was that same set of advice that gave me the confidence to open my own public relations company after just under a decade in the business, and that guides me through until today.

I have tried to pay this forward to my kids in terms of word and demonstration, and though it has been emotionally difficult at each juncture, giving roots and wings is just one of those things you have to do so that your children can grow to be their best selves.

Helping our kids learn self-reliance is exhausting, thrilling, and heartbreaking, all at the same time. BUT, if we've done our job well, they will have the fortitude and experience to live a happy life, make us proud, and pay the wisdom that they have learned forward to the next generation.

Remember:

- Gentle and consistent persistence pays off
- Encourage your kids to follow their dreams as far as they can take them
- Even when it's frustrating, remember that your kids' persistence can demonstrate conviction and dedication
- Share your personal stories and memories to create an additional connection with your children and help them to better understand you

- Rest easier knowing your kids have you in the back of their minds as they embark on their own journeys

If you would like to practice applying the public relations strategies above to your own story, please use your cell phone camera to scan the QR code below or use the hyperlink to access the free workbook that will walk you through the process.
https://prfor.life/the-power-of-pr-parenting-login-page-qr/

CHAPTER 8

SHOWING UP

In this chapter:

- Being available, even when inconvenient
- Showing up—in person or by proxy
- Using little patterns to create a positive space
- Leveraging your superpowers

In public relations, all clients want to feel like they are your one and only and that they have access to you whenever they need. And when you are working with clients in multiple time zones, which is the norm in international PR, this often leads to literally 24/7 availability.

For my favorites, though, I've gone that extra mile even beyond the time zone thing.

Answering the Call, ALWAYS

One fine evening before Maya was born, and when Noa Lee and Guy were little and already in bed, I was in the bathtub, warming my bones and relaxing from the day's roller-coaster ride at the big agency. The room was full of luxurious steam. I was floating in my imagination when my husband opened the bathroom door. A gust of cold air broke through the steam and my bubble of serenity.

"The hotel lady is on the phone," he whispered. "Do you want to take it?"

I didn't need to think about it. I instantly replied, "Yes," as I stretched my hand out to accept the phone. The "hotel lady" was one of my favorite clients—smart, no-nonsense, stylish, and fun. She was also a power gal executive, and I had enormous respect for her work. If she needed something, I was always available.

The hotel lady and I chatted about whatever was on her mind for about a half an hour before I told her that I would need to break and call her back. She inquired why.

"It's just that I'm in the bath, and the water is cold now," I said with a chuckle. "Let me dry off, get dressed, and I'll call you right back."

She laughed. If she hadn't before, she now understood just how VIP she was in my book and how truly available I was when she needed me.

This is not a unique situation—not the bathtub part, but the availability part. PR professionals regularly drop whatever they are doing, at any moment, even if just for a few moments, to acknowledge a request or to service an immediate need of a client.

For some reason, these calls always seemed to come after hours and during afternoon carpool time, when I was taking the kids and their friends to their various activities.

I had a *deeboreet* (car speaker in Hebrew) and would answer while waiting for the kids or driving—of course, both hands on the wheel and eyes on the road.

"Hi! This is Marjie. How are you? Just want you to know that I am driving with a full car of kids who can hear you. If you need to share something confidential, let me call you back. If not, we are all ears."

Some cared and deferred the call. Others didn't and greeted the kids. For their part, the kids thought the whole thing was fun from the start and returned the courtesy before going quiet. They and their friends knew that if I got a work call, it was quiet time until the call was over.

"Shhh, shhh, everyone, Mommy's on a call!"

Now, let's ask ourselves a very important question: If we, and even our kids, prioritize like this for our clients or bosses, then why shouldn't we do the same for our kids? Whenever they call us or need our attention, and it doesn't matter when, doesn't it make sense to drop everything for a moment to see what's up, what is SOOOO important, and perhaps why they think the sky might be falling?

It might be something small, like when I was in Tianjin, China attending the World Economic Forum with a client. I had just arrived, and thanks to jetlag and the concrete-hard bed in the hotel room, it took until 3:00 a.m. to fall asleep. Not too much later, my mobile phone rang. It was little Maya, then five years old.

"Hi Mommy," she said.

"Hi Love. What's up? Everything okay?" I asked, checking the time on my phone. I had been asleep for only 15 minutes. Oy vey.

"Can I watch TV?" she inquired.

"Is your father at home?" I replied.

"Yes," Maya confirmed.

"Ask him to help you please, Darling. Mommy loves you. I'm happy to hear from you. And now I'm going back to sleep."

"Okay, Mommy. I love you," she declared. I heard her shout, "Daddy!" before she hung up.

Or it might be something potentially huge that could influence their future if we don't make ourselves instantly available to help.

This happened once when Isaac and I were visiting my mother and my younger sister and her family in Florida. We were at the end of a three-week East Coast trip inspired by two family weddings. Our kids had remained at home to attend classes and study. Guy and Noa Lee were legal adults by then, and Maya was also at an age where she could legally be left alone, though she had Guy and Noa Lee in the event of an issue. They were self-sufficient and had the use of our credit card and cars. All good. Right?

It was 4:00 a.m. Eastern Time on a Sunday. The sun was sleeping and so were we when my mobile phone rang and its blue light cast a cold glow in the dark and otherwise warm and cozy bedroom at my sister's place.

I answered, half awake.

"Mommy, I need your help urgently," a voice sobbed with frustration.

"What's wrong, Maya?" I replied, trying to race to full alertness, 0 to 60 in a matter of seconds.

"I need you to make me a blood test appointment for tomorrow, and there's no room. And if I don't get one then I won't have what I need for my first army interview in time, and the process will be delayed by at least six months," she explained between tears.

Before we had left for our trip, we had booked Maya for the Tuesday of that week for a blood test, but, as it turns out, it wasn't good enough.

To her credit, Maya had tried to reschedule this appointment herself, but there were no appointments for the next day, Monday, in our neighborhood at the health group we belonged to, and the administrator refused to help with a squeeze-in.

"Maya, give me a couple of seconds to wake up. It's 4 a.m.," I replied, sounding a little irked.

"Mommy, you said I could call you any time of day or night if I needed," she asserted.

She was right. That's what I had said. And I meant it. I was available in the middle of the night to service client calls. Why NOT my own kid?

It was now 4:10 a.m. ET, which meant it was 11:10 a.m. in Israel. The health group would close for work at 1 p.m. Israel time. No time to waste, and indeed it was time to step up.

I called and did my PR/Mama bear thing—repeating several times why an appointment the next day was crucial and that it HAD to be the next day. The administrator finally asked me for Maya's ID and said, "Tell her to be here tomorrow at 9:30 a.m.," before slamming the phone down in my ear.

I called Maya back with the good news. She exhaled, and her voice and volume returned to normal.

Noa Lee accompanied Maya to her blood test the next day. Maya was one of several squeeze-ins at the clinic that morning, and though she needed to maneuver on her own a bit more on-site, she achieved her goal. Maya received and sent the test results on time to the army. This time it worked out. It doesn't always, but in all cases, the kids knew I was there if they needed me to step up.

Yup, parenthood and PR—two 24/7 jobs that don't let up. Your job too?

Prioritizing and Sourcing Your Team

Being available 24/7 for two 24/7 jobs, work and parenthood, as all working parents know, is easier said than done.

You've got to work to earn the money to feed your family, and let's just go ahead and admit it, advance our careers, which also benefits our children.

BUT, we also have to show up for our kid/s to make new memories, invest in bonding time, and reinforce our commitment to them. When work and school schedules conflict, we ask ourselves, what on earth are we supposed to do to keep everyone happy?

At PR agencies, there are teams of people to service each account and consultants have a network of freelancers to support work activity as needed. No one HAS to do everything themselves, especially if they are willing to delegate or if they have a colleague who has their back in times of need.

The same applies to family. In this parallel, your family team is your partner, parent, grandparent, sibling, or anyone else who your child loves and trusts. Any of these people can provide some substitution on your behalf, including at school and after-school events. There's nothing worse than being the kid in the room with no one there.

Clearly, if you can get backup at work, then do so, because the best way to be present for your kids boils down to showing up—in person or virtually. But if that's impossible, no judgment. We all do the best we can. Just make sure to back yourself up.

It's very important to remember that years from now our kids are the ones who will be taking care of us when we are old—not our colleagues, not our bosses, and not our clients, all of whom may be long out of our lives by then.

If we are thinking long-term, why would our kids prioritize us if we don't prioritize them? Our kids learn from our being present or lack of being present and pay it forward.

When I think about investing in our children by showing up in large and small ways for them, Harry Chapin's song "Cat's in the Cradle" comes to mind as, to me, it musically expresses the truth that you often reap from your children what you sow. A line in one of the verses is a sad, but perfect example of this. The senior citizen dad in the song calls his now grown son and asks to see him. His son replies:

"...I'd love to, dad, if I could find the time...."

After they hang up, the dad realizes that his son had grown up exactly like him. He hadn't prioritized his son while he was growing up, and now the son, without malice but also without much thought, is not prioritizing his father in his long list of daily responsibilities.

So whenever possible, just like you would for clients, do what you can to show up for your child's big moment in the spotlight, to see their art displayed on the school hallway wall, to hear them sing or play their instrument, or to participate in a parent-child bonding activity. It makes a huge difference for them, and your being there teaches them the importance of being there in the future for their kids, for you, and for others important in their life.

Now, I am not a self-declared supermom. Far, FAR from it. I'd sneak quick emails and texts during school events, and I didn't join one field trip until Maya was in her last year of elementary school, mainly because I was concerned that my limited and accented Hebrew would infringe upon helping to manage the needs and safety of the class on any given adventure. Turns out, it was all in my head, and the older two resented me for this for years. I wasn't present when they felt they needed me in these cases, even though it wasn't because of work, but because of fear.

For the events I did attend, though, I was in classic PR mom form, with camera and video recorder in hand, striving for the best shot in a sea of parents, pushing to the front of the pack like the paparazzi. And if I had the better angle, I'd also record my friends' kids and send them the footage later.

From my experience, our kids see us in the audience clicking away, looking for that perfect shot, and light up knowing we are there for them, and they are the center of our universe at that moment. Our attention is solely on our child, and they drink this up like a cool glass of lemonade on a hot summer day. What could be better than having Mommy all to themselves, basking in her love, approval, and validation? This attention filled my kids, and their happiness filled me. I'm sure you know what I mean.

Look, our days will ALWAYS be busy, so we need to time manage and do our best to squeeze it all in and make the seemingly impossible possible, like in PR when there are minutes to go until a publicly traded company press release is legally supposed to be submitted to NASDAQ for disclosure and then cross the paid newswire, and the client calls with one last little change and asks, "Can you?"

When I'd get calls like this, I'd look at the clock and think, can I do this with this amount of time?

For the sake of argument, let's say I had five minutes until the press release was to post, which wasn't an uncommon time frame for such requests.

I'd think: *60 seconds to flag the wire service contact. Another 60 seconds to make the requested copy change. Another 60 seconds to send the updated copy to the wire service contact. And another 60 seconds to submit to NASDAQ. Cool. I can get it done with one minute to spare. Go. Go. Go!*

High pressure? Yes. Impossible? No. So, I drove the poor people at the wire service crazy and added some white hair to my already prematurely white "do" (which began to turn when I was 29). BUT my client was happy, so I was happy.

Now, how do we apply this lesson to being more present for our kids, even when every ball seems like it's up in the air, and it feels like we don't have an extra second to spare in the day?

Try this:

See one week as seven days, a day as 24 hours, an hour as 60 minutes, and see one minute as 60 seconds.

Now, let's think together, what do you need to do this week? Overwhelming, right?

So, let's just take one day—at a time. Use a daily organizer or just a pad of paper to lists things out if it helps.

What do you need to do tomorrow? Just tomorrow. That's big picture enough for now.

Now, let's take that first hour of the day tomorrow. What does that look like? You have six blocks of 10 minutes. Or if your activities each go really quickly, maybe you have up to 60 blocks of time or more. All of a sudden, one hour seems like a lot of time.

If you think about it, it's amazing how much can be done in 60 minutes rather than one hour. If you look at it this way, you may find time you didn't realize you had for what's important to you. And frankly, we are women. We are gifted with being able to do more than one thing at a time, which means we can squeeze even more into any given day.

Think about what we can do with a few extra seconds. How about telling your child for the millionth time how much you love them and are proud? In my opinion, you can't do these things enough, even if they pretend to protest—Oh, Mom!

Creating a Positive Presence

PR people are generally rather friendly people. We smile a lot—with our facial expressions and with our tone of voice. It's part of the job, even when we feel terrible or are in the worst mood. I have found that even if I don't "feel like it" some days, if I put a smile on my face, the day instantly starts to improve.

At work, just to be pleasant and give a good feeling, I would smile at a colleague passing by or a client if we'd make eye contact.

No matter my disposition, I also tried to create a pleasant and good feeling at home. I'd not only smile at the kids when we'd make eye contact, but I'd also make myself available for that little extra—a big hug. I think this might be the way that I have been most present and available to my kids.

When my children were babies, I hugged them all the time and would hold them close to me on my lap, even as I would type away with my right hand on my keyboard. They played with a small toy as they nestled into mommy, wrapped in my left arm.

There was always a big bear hug during drop-off and then again at pick-up from the kindergarten and elementary school. Sometimes the kids would literally run over and jump into my arms, both of us with big smiles on our faces as we reunited.

At home during these same years, my kids used to *knock mommy over* as I was sitting on the couch and then giggle at their seemingly overwhelming display of strength, all the while giving and getting a bear hug.

As the years went on, if they'd say, "Mommy, I want a hug." Or ask, "Mommy, can I have a hug?" I'd stop whatever I was doing to hug them, and they'd do the same whenever I'd make the same request.

And sometimes they would just give me or Isaac a hug out of nowhere.

Yup, lots of hugging going on at our house. And I, for one, LOVED it! I still do.

I have found that in these moments, we bask in the warmth of this unconditional love.

Today, even though my kids are young adults, hugs remain a part of our natural interaction. Hugs dissipate any hurt or self-doubt, fortify any triumph, and serve as an injection of positive energy.

In fact, there are scientific studies that show that a 20-second hug can help calm us down, improve our health and disposition, as well as provide several other positive benefits. It's not scientific as far as I know, but I also wait for my child to release the hug first before I let go. This way, they get what they need—sometimes more, sometimes less than 20 seconds. And during hug time, everything else can wait.

Whether it's a hug, an arm around a shoulder, a smile, or a wink, these couple of seconds of physical or visual contact can mean everything to your kids and make them feel acknowledged, important, and loved.

No money required, only seconds of your time to get this positive energy going back and forth, and then both you and your child can reap the priceless and long-term rewards.

So, let's stop a moment here and get you in on this. If your kids are reasonably nearby, please put down this book and take a break from reading for a moment. Please find your child or children and offer them a hug and if they accept, then hug them comfortably for 20 seconds, unless, of course, they release earlier.

Tell them you love them and that you are proud of them. If they ask, "Why?" tell them, "I'm proud because I like you and the kind of person you are." Then, come back to this book, and let's continue our conversation. I'll be here waiting for you. If they aren't around at the moment, keep reading, but make sure to exercise this request at the next opportunity.

If you went to hug your child(ren), how did it go? What was their reaction? How did you feel? Did it make a small but positive difference in your day?

My guess is yes. And if so, I'd suggest repeating this exercise every day and multiple times a day. It's good for the kids, and it's good for us, too.

Celebrating Milestones

In PR, we are always encouraged to think outside of the box when creating press strategies and creating events. It got me thinking: *Why not apply the same approach to my kids' birthday parties? They are events too, right?*

Yes, a cake, a present, and a birthday song can certainly be enough. But thinking outside of the box and making something special can be more exciting for the birthday child and their friends.

How? Take your cue from your kids and acknowledge their special day by planning a celebration that reflects their personality and that will fill them with joy.

While brainstorming just how to do this, think about your own superpowers. How can you take what you are best at and use it to augment (not upstage!) your child's happiness?

One year during the kindergarten days, I asked if I could hire a clown to entertain the kids for Noa Lee's birthday. The answer was no. No outside anyone. Thinking outside of the box, I asked if I could dress up as a clown and entertain the kids myself. The answer was yes. If I were crazy enough to do it, I was invited.

I thought: *For my girl, I am willing to make a fool of myself.*

I arrived in full clown wardrobe—a pillow strapped to my abdomen and dressed in X-Large, unmatching checkered clothing. My hair was tied in multiple little colorful ponytail holders all over my head, and my face was painted with multiple colors, including an oversized, bright pink lipstick smile. I made a big and loud entrance as I arrived at Noa Lee's kindergarten, picked up my then three-year-old daughter, first hugged her tightly, and then swung her around the room.

We then turned on some music, and I danced with all the kids in her class and delivered a birthday cake iced with a Disney image. Noa Lee, wearing her favorite Snow White dress from a Disney store, was thrilled.

Mommy didn't just show up; Mommy brought the party. And all it cost me was a little bit of pride.

After the party, it was time to pick up Guy from elementary school. No time to change or clean off the face makeup. You can just imagine the surprised faces of the kids and the teachers, all who wanted to know, "Where's the party???"

Guy simply smiled, understanding it was Noa Lee's birthday and enjoying the spotlight a little too that day. Yes, his mom is a little crazy, but she's also good fun.

To this day, Noa Lee and Guy remember this afternoon with smiles and love. I may not have been the best clown, but they appreciated the effort and my out-of-the-box demonstration of my commitment to their happiness. This commitment is something we all share as parents.

Now I'd like to ask you to think out of the box. What's your superpower? Cooking? Baking? Art? Playing an instrument? Languages? Impressions? Making funny sounds? Chess? Gymnastics?

And which of these superpowers does your child also share a love for?

Plan an activity around this for your child's next birthday. Whether you are good at it or not really doesn't matter. (I was a terrible clown, and the kids still loved it!) Invite your child to join you in doing this thing that you both love and celebrate with joy TOGETHER.

Happy mommy, happy kids.
Happy kids, happy mommy.

Being Present Everyday

At our house, mommy's attention mostly came between 4 p.m. and 8 p.m., between daycare or school pick up and bedtime. During these hours, sometimes I would drive them to a playdate or host one and hang out with the other mothers as our kids played in front of our gaze. In later years, I would drive them to an activity like judo or dance class and watch them from an observation window.

On other days, we would return home for a snack and a dance party. I have always loved to sing and dance. I'd never make the Broadway stage, so my living room would just have to do. To the best of Motown, Carole King, Miami Sound Machine, Broadway musicals, and Disney movie soundtracks (to name a few), we'd sing, jump, dip, twirl and skip in delight. And whoever came to visit on any given day joined in the fun. There was always plenty of spaghetti or pizza and salad.

Perhaps you have kids of varying ages and taking care of the babies is a priority in the afternoons. Though you can sing and dance with the baby in your arms, sometimes changing a diaper or feeding time takes priority. All good, make a game out of it and include the older ones in the childcare by assigning them a helper's task. It's fun, inclusive, and it helps you to start building your home team, which you may recall from Chapter 1, may be crucially important in the future.

"Timmy, you are in charge of the diaper cream. Could you please bring it to me? Excellent job!"

"Sally, you are in charge of the diapers. Please have one ready and slip it under your baby sister's tush. Perfect. Well done!"

If you are making dinner, invite your kids to measure out the ingredients, add them to the various dishes, and set the table. And, early on, assign them household chores and teach them to always clean up their mess, and any other mess they might happen to notice. Otherwise, this will be on you until the end of eternity. Follow me?

The daily grind doesn't have to be a daily grind, it can be a fun family activity, and you can build a support system along the way.

Bottom line: Our kids want to be part of our world, see us smile, laugh, and enjoy with them.

Guy, Noa Lee, and I were recently standing in the kitchen. I was getting a coffee when Guy asked me if I was fun, or old and boring.

I held my head high, smiled, and declared: "FUN!"

Then he played a video of an opera singer and asked if he could record me singing what I remembered of the song I had just heard. I agreed.

In my best soprano, which borders on squeaky and sounds much like a doggy squeeze toy, I sang, "Uh uh uh uh uh." Then he played my ridiculous-sounding recording back.

I laughed. They laughed. Happiness all around and all in good fun. I was present in that moment with them, eye contact and all, and they soaked it in—so much that they both hugged me right after. Amazing payoff. The whole interaction took maybe five minutes or 300 seconds. And what a wonderful 300 seconds it was.

Remember:

- Tell your kids you're there for them 24/7 and mean it; if you set boundaries (like in the car), they will reciprocate
- Don't let your kid be the one without someone showing up
- Organize your day by compartmentalizing the hours and minutes
- Build a reliable bench of loved ones who can step in
- Don't just be present—use little moments to make that presence a positive one
- Use what you love to do to make your child's experiences happier

If you would like to practice applying the public relations strategies above to your own story, please use your cell phone camera to scan the QR code below or use the hyperlink to access the free workbook that will walk you through the process.
https://prfor.life/the-power-of-pr-parenting-login-page-qr/

CHAPTER 9

DEADLINES AND SELF-CARE

In this chapter:

- Using strategies, tactics, and deadlines to achieve goals
- Applying time management to the teenage years
- Meeting deadlines to show respect
- Encouraging your child to go the distance
- Acknowledging that Mommy Time is a Want AND A Need

For publicists, deadlines are a daily reality, with some being timed down to the split second, like when you have booked your client for a live TV interview.

"3...2...1...cue the talent!"

There is also the quick turnaround deadline, when you need to draft a press release or a fact sheet summarizing the happenings, findings, or agreements from a live event, literally, as the event is occurring or just at its conclusion, get it approved on-site and then, as they say, "out the door", meaning distributed to the press and the public ASAP. No turning back.

There are due dates and deadlines for everything: client proposals, press materials, answers for the press, content for social media postings, website launches, collateral materials... the list goes on. And my kids had a front-row seat for decades to how seriously I took the whole thing and how I time managed to make countless deadlines. Our kids are always watching.

But it's not just in PR. We all face the dreaded but inevitable deadline, and all of us are held accountable no matter our profession.

We also have deadlines imposed by our personal circumstances, by our family, friends, and even the random stranger.

"Will that be cash or credit?" the cashier asks. The deadline to pay has arrived.

In the perfect world, we'd have one deadline at a time, and we would only need to focus on one finish line at a time. But the world is perfectly imperfect, and we are faced with multiple deadlines every day and sometimes at the same moment. Oy vey!

How do we time manage it all?

The first thing I do with a new client is ask them what their short-, medium- and long-term goals are. Once these are defined, we then work backwards and devise the strategies and the supporting tactics that we will implement to help achieve these goals by the designated deadlines. We also define those very important key messages that we have discussed throughout the book.

Once defined, we loosely put each of the strategies and tactics on a timeline and map them out on a shared calendar. The calendar is a rolling and dynamic one, which often changes to reflect current events, new realities, and adjusted goals.

Then it's time to implement. Among my functions is to be the timekeeper by regularly and repeatedly reminding my clients where we are in the timeline and what remains outstanding and pending. We give lots of gentle reminders to keep things moving forward, including right up to the last minutes, like just before those live TV interviews.

When we meet a deadline and with good work, we have a feeling of accomplishment, and sometimes let out a sigh of relief, as we can now check that action item off our list, and hopefully, with a "job well done" attached to it. We take a few minutes to enjoy the win, and then it's on to the next deadline.

If we miss a deadline, we might lose credibility, respect, and accountability in the eyes of our boss, client, or colleagues. In severe cases, perhaps we lose a client, job, or coveted opportunity.

We all want to make those deadlines with good work and be winners, and we want to teach our kids to do the same and to achieve and experience some level of success along the way too.

Now, how do we apply this public relations practice to parenting?

Let's start with the goals. Goals can pertain to anything of interest, including the big things like academics, extracurriculars, and good nutrition, as well as the smaller things like keeping their room clean, walking the dog, and helping around the house.

Let's further break this down using academics as our example.

I think we can all agree that our big picture goal is for our children to learn as much as possible, apply these learnings to a future career, and become financially independent adults contributing in a positive way to society.

For the purpose of this exercise, though, let's concentrate on the generally universal reality associated with achieving such a big-picture goal—getting good grades. Yes, there are exceptions to the rule, but for now, let's focus on the rule.

Beginning in first grade and in every grade and educational program thereafter, the kids have a list of courses to take and subjects to study.

The long-term academic goal is for your child to get good (or good enough) grades in all of their courses so that they have the required average at the end of each school year to advance to the next academic level the following term, eventually graduate, and ultimately go on to higher education and/or a successful career. In Israel, remember, there's military service first.

The medium-term academic goal is for your child to get good grades on their midterms and finals, which will help achieve the long-term goal.

And the short-term academic goal is to do well on the little tests and quizzes along the way, turn in their completed papers, projects, and homework on time, punctually show up for class—in person or online with the camera on—and participate.

Next, the academic strategy: It can help to plan a home study schedule to achieve each of the above goals.

Pull out a hardcopy or an electronic calendar, or perhaps an app on their phone where they can get alerts and chart together test days and when the homework, papers, and projects are due.

First, you record the entries, but if they are old enough to write or type, then quickly hand over the reins to your child so that they can gain control of the activity and establish some independence and ownership of the time management/deadline exercise.

Maybe set aside an hour or more each day to go over the homework while reserving ample time to practice any subject that needs reinforcing. Encourage your child to take a short break every 20 minutes if needed. I do.

Also, when it's test time, one subject might take priority over another and require more time that week to best prepare for the medium-term academic goal. If you see your child is struggling and needs more time with one subject and less with another, then adjust the timeline as needed.

The timeline is dynamic and not written in stone. It's whatever works best for your child and will help them make their deadlines with success. It's not about pressure; it's about giving a loose structure to help your child happily want to stay on course, kind of like bowling lane bumpers.

Everyone Learns Differently

Tactics: Everybody learns differently. Does your child learn better when listening to the teacher or when seeing the teacher write on the board? If your child favors one or the other, consider that when supporting their practice and homework assignments at home or with additional assistance from the school or from tutors, whether professional or a family member or friend.

Even though we all need to know how to handwrite, sometimes some of us are more comfortable with typing, whereas others prefer to use a pen or a pencil. Being able to use our preference can help make doing homework and taking tests a little easier and a bit more enjoyable. Something to consider and discuss with your child and your child's teacher.

How long can your child maintain concentration on each subject? This should factor into your time allocation. And is your child a slow or fast reader? If slow, block out a little extra time to help them get through the assigned pages.

These are just a few things to consider as you are planning the tactics that could help your child to achieve their short, medium, and long-term goals.

Help them to plan it all out as well as answer questions and support them by regularly, but gently, asking them where they are in their timeline: "How's the studying coming along?"

Sometimes I'd get a little more aggressive, "You have a test coming up, right? How are you time managing?"

Eventually, time management and making deadlines will not only become an accepted, natural process for your child, but also a respected one in the long term.

On test day, I'd wish them good luck.

If they had indeed time managed properly and studied well, then hopefully, they'd be able to do their best, and that's always good enough for me. Can't do better than your best.

If they came home with a good test grade or a good report card, the house was full of joy from their success. Everyone prefers to get it right the first time.

If they came home with a bad grade on a test, I'd remind them that it wasn't about the battle but about the war. Everyone has a bad test, even a bad report card, and we were in it for the long haul. That was generally enough feedback as they were already disappointed and beating themselves up about it.

If this happens to your child, empathize. Just like I tell my clients to keep their answers positive, even when presented with pointedly negative interview questions, I'm also suggesting that you keep your responses positive, especially with the negative energy of disappointment from your child staring you straight in the face. Remember that your kid truly does want to succeed.

Sometimes it will work out, and sometimes it won't, even with their best effort. Again, we need to encourage our kids to keep trying and pursue their long-term goals as far as they can go, understanding that there may be roadblocks along the way.

Let's take Noa Lee as an example. Her long-term academic goal was to go to a top medical school in an exciting city that would ultimately enable her to practice just about anywhere in the world. But remember the 11th grade disaster year we talked about in Chapter 4 when we discussed contracts? Though she had scored very well on her tests, the teachers docked her for her lack of attendance, and her graduating grade point average suffered from that.

It didn't stop her though from pursuing her ambition. She just adjusted her strategy. After she was released from the army, she took an intensive course that prepares students to take the required exams for select medical schools with their own set of very difficult entry tests. By this point, goals, strategy, and tactics came naturally to Noa Lee, and she had her eyes firmly set on the donut.

BINGO! She got the job done and was accepted to her first choice of medical school, which is in one of the most beautiful cities in the world. It wasn't an easy journey and certainly not a straight line, but she achieved her long-term academic goal despite the hiccups along the way.

As for Isaac and me, we intervened during the high school years as needed, but while Noa Lee was prepping for the medical school exams, we did our best to just stay out of the way and encourage her as much as possible to go the distance.

We continue to do this with all three of our kids.

Guy, who, as you know, did well in high school, but not well enough for what he wanted to study in college, again, also found a way to make the grade and be accepted into the elite university program of his choice. And though Maya's story is still being written, we have faith in her too, as we watch her discover what works for her and what doesn't, reassess strategy, and both time manage, and study differently based on her new strategy.

I encourage you, too, to keep the faith and inspire your child to do the same.

Together, if necessary, reconsider your strategy and plan in order for your child to study better for the next set of tests. Not harder—trust that they are already studying hard and, at this point, are frustrated. What they need to do is find a new and more constructive study path that will lead them to success—the best reward of all.

Perhaps assign specific times to execute this new study strategy. If they have consistently learned in a way suitable for them and are well prepared, then come test day, remind them, "Yes, you've got this!"

Encourage them to take a deep breath and do their thing. Hopefully, the report card grade will reflect their efforts. And if not, nothing happened. Encourage them to keep trying until they find a way that enables them to cross the finish line triumphantly. Offer assistance and be available if they ask for help with this. Most importantly, keep the comments constructive and optimistic. In my experience, they'll be more likely to believe they can succeed if you show them that you believe they can with your words, tone, and facial expressions.

As time passes, the kids will have the whole process down and can manage it themselves, at least this has been my experience.

For example, Guy and I were watching TV together on the couch, enjoying a little mother-son time during his first semester in university.

About a half an hour into watching, I asked him to pause the show.

"Don't you have a final exam next week?" I inquired.

"Yes, but don't worry, I'm time managing," he replied.

He then clicked play on the TV remote and resumed the show. When it was over, around 20 minutes later, he returned to his room to continue studying and preparing for the test.

I smiled to myself, thinking—mission accomplished.

The Teenage Years

The teenage years are when the deadline conversation adjusts to include: "Okay, so you are going out tonight? Where? With whom? Remember: curfew is at 12 midnight, not 12:01 a.m., 12 midnight."

Just like I'd ping my clients ten minutes before a scheduled press interview was about to take place to make sure they knew showtime was looming, I also messaged my kids around 20 minutes before curfew that their coach was about to turn into a pumpkin.

Was I annoying to them? ABSOLUTELY.

But at the stroke of midnight, I'd hear the front door open and close. "I'm home!" they'd shout.

And when they weren't going to arrive on time, more often than not, they'd message me about their delay, including where they were, why they would be late, and their estimated time of arrival. So, at least there were expectations, and there was no need to worry.

I pinged the kids until they were 18. Once they were legal adults, then I just wanted to be informed when I should expect them to walk through the door. For safety reasons only, and I've said this before, there should always be someone at your last stop of the day who knows when to expect you. And as long as my kids were living at home, that one person was me.

Deadline Respect Is Symbiotic

Respecting deadlines is part of having a strong work ethic as well as a way of being considerate to the time management of others.

Mommy and Daddy must make their deadlines to get the job done so they can earn their paycheck. The kids need to make their deadlines at school to help achieve good grades so they can ultimately get into college if they so choose. And deadlines must be honored at home in the form of curfews, so Mommy and Daddy can go to sleep without concern.

To this day, deadlines are taken seriously, even if on occasion, they are missed for one reason or another, most times legitimate.

How about at your house? Are your kids time managing well and respecting the deadlines at home and at school?

It's always nice to hear it from them first. But sometimes, if they are not volunteering, then perhaps it's best to ask.

First, prepare yourself by creating what we call in public relations a Question and Answer (Q&A) document. We create these for our clients to prepare them for interviews. The gist of it here is to anticipate the answers your child might give to your questions and to be ready with follow-up questions to get to the bottom of whatever issue there might be, assuming there is an issue. All might be just fine, too.

Listen carefully to their answers to your questions and encourage them to elaborate along the way.

I always start with:

"How are you?"

The answer could be: "Stressed." If so, ask: "Why?"

The answer could be: "Okay." If so, perhaps reply: "Cool. Tell me more. What's okay?"

The answer could be: "Great!" If so, reply: "Fantastic. Tell me what's great. I'm interested."

The answer could be: "Everything sucks." Then empathize: "I understand. What sucks?"

Follow up with some open-ended questions like:

"Tell me about school?"

"Tell me about (insert extra-curricular activity)?"

"Tell me about your friends and what's happening there?"

And some closed questions like: "What tests are coming up? How are you time managing?" (Yes, use these exact words—time managing.)

And lastly: "Anything I can help with?"

Suppose they say: "No." Then perhaps reply with: "I'm not trying to stress you out or add any pressure. If you need my help, all you have to do is ask, and I'll be there for you."

If and when they do come to you, explain first that, just like preproduction is important to planning a successful event (Chapter 3), so too is time management to meet those short- and medium-term deadlines. It's basically the same concept with different window dressing, and it applies to just about everything we do in life.

When my kids got older, sometimes they'd be forthcoming when I'd start this line of questioning. Sometimes they'd shut me out. I respected their boundaries and waited until the moment arrived when they were ready to have a discussion, which sometimes came at unexpected times, like very, very late at night or during a car ride. I'd listen, recommend some courses of action if invited to do so, and then they'd take it from there.

The most important thing is to try to be patient with your kids and with yourself at each stage of this habitual process. No one is 100%, 100% of the time. Not us and not our kids. And it takes lots of practice to excel both at time management and making deadlines. But it will happen. Believe.

Prioritizing Self-care... Yes, Really

We've talked about how to teach time management and respecting deadlines to kids, now let's turn the spotlight on you.

Self-care is one of the action items working parents have the hardest time booking in their schedules and honoring as a real deadline. For some reason, self-care always seems to take second chair or get deleted altogether.

And yet, this may be the most important line item on your list. Happier mommy, happier kids. I know that my kids always smile a little more when they see me in a good place. And yours will too. And remember, they will follow your lead someday based on your example. This is a good thing. We want our kids to take good care of themselves, present and future.

So, PLEASE consider self-care a priority when time managing your day, week, month, and year, keeping in mind that self-care can take many shapes and forms, some universal, some personal, but in ALL cases, they are not only a WANT but also a NEED.

Let's start with the universal: rest.

Before we were parents, the question was: Are you tired? After you joined the ranks of parenthood, the more appropriate question became: How tired are you?

We go, go, go like energizer bunnies. But we all have batteries, and if not charged regularly and properly, we'll burn out, especially with our crazy schedules, insane list of to-dos, and exhausting amounts of responsibilities.

I'll share how this PR pro got through it and how I still get through it until today: the power nap.

Hallelujah, the power nap!!

Many times, I would be sitting at my desk, drafting something, when the words would start running into each other on the screen. I was soooo tired. I felt my eyes closing, and my body aching to rest. When I'm THAT tired, I start to work in slo-mo, going nowhere fast, and know that it's best just to stop and rest before I do something stupid or cause damage.

When I felt this way, whether at the agency or at my home office, I would put my head back on my work chair, close my eyes, and doze off for around 10, sometimes 20 minutes. It is well documented that these 10-20 minutes can be highly beneficial in terms of reinvigoration.

From my experience, and I think we can agree, moms never quite fall asleep 100%, even in the middle of the night. We always have one ear open for trouble. The same goes for the power nap. BUT it's still a nap, and enough to recharge your battery and give you that needed power to do a great job on whatever the next deadline is, with full clarity, and to make it through the rest of the day, deadline after deadline, with a smile on your face.

If someone saw me with my eyes closed at the office and questioned me about it, I'd say I was working out an idea in my head—which was true. I also used my naps to work out what I needed to do next. When I opened my eyes to look at the time, I would recalculate the time I had to finish my tactics connected to the strategy and figure how quickly or slowly I should work to meet the deadline.

At home, by the time the kids might interrupt my power nap, I was already recharged.

I invite you now to sample the power nap. And if you are already familiar, to enjoy another. It's my gift to you. Put this book down. Put your head back. Close your eyes and take the next 10 to 20 minutes to breathe and sleep a little. I'll be waiting for you when you wake up.

Using "Me Time" to Present Yourself at Your Best

How was your nap? Good, I hope. Let's continue.

Now, let's talk about a personalized type of self-care.

When you prepare your clients for a TV interview or an online video presentation, hair, makeup, and wardrobe are always worked into the agenda and considered part of the deadline schedule. Sometimes a professional is hired; other times, clients pull it together a little more than they usually would on their own.

Why is this important? Glamor is part of visually presenting yourself professionally, giving your best show, and properly representing your company.

When we have glammed up, we know we are looking our best, and when we are looking our best, we stand a little taller and feel that little bit more confident because we took the time to take care of ourselves—emphasis on the taking care of ourselves part, not so much on the glamming up, even though glamming up is fun too.

Now, wouldn't it be nice if we could take good care of ourselves every day? Not just for TV interviews or special occasions? And I don't mean just hair, makeup, and wardrobe. I mean time managing a little *me time* each week to be nice to yourself. I can't emphasize how important this is, even with a wicked busy schedule.

How? First, make the time, sister! If you have time to shower and brush your teeth every day, you can squeeze a little more in for some *me time* somewhere. Just put it in the calendar and honor your commitment to yourself.

Me time can be defined however you wish. Just make it something that you like to do, frees you from your daily routine, and refreshes your inner core.

There will be days when this simply feels impossible. That's okay. Perhaps on those days, take an extra minute or two in the shower to enjoy the hot water or a little extra time during a bathroom break to breathe and shut your eyes. It's all good.

For me, I started every day by time managing a little *me time* with an extra five minutes of sleep in the morning after the alarm went off and reassigned pulling myself together to later in the day.

In the early years, when the kids were really little and just after I had started working remotely from home, I began organizing myself AFTER school drop-off.

I'd roll out of bed, wash my hands and face, brush my teeth and hair (90 seconds), dash down the stairs, and go straight to preparing them and serving the breakfasts, and packing the bag lunches. I made sure they had water bottles, and then it was out the door—my hair in a ponytail, dressed in sweats, and no makeup. I looked so UN-put together that the other parents asked me on occasion if I worked.

That made me laugh. "I work around the clock and usually end my day at 1 a.m." I'd chuckle.

"Oh!" they'd say, astonished.

Hmmm, the judgment. I cared NOT. Not from them and not from anyone else who may have seen me on any given morning looking like the Bride of Frankenstein (lucky Isaac!).

That was MY way of delivering self-care from the moment I woke up. I wanted that extra sleep time, and I was prepared to pay the early morning glamor bill for it.

Clearly, if I had to go into an office just after drop-off, I would get up a little earlier and become professional looking before, rather than after, the morning rush. More times than not, though, I'd bring my makeup with me to the meeting and glam up before leaving the car, using the rearview mirror, which for some reason always seemed to have the perfect light for this.

On a daily basis, though, I took my time, enjoyed an hour of quiet at the top of the day after drop-off, and scheduled my first meeting in person or by video conference for 11 a.m. or after.

In my opinion, rule number one in self-care for the working mom is to pull it together only as much as is required, only as much as you feel needed at any given moment, and only as much as you WANT to. There are some days, frankly, when I just don't feel like it. And so I don't. And that's okay too.

We need to carve out *me time*, whether that means pushing forward your morning wake-up deadline or booking an appointment at your local hair salon so you'll have a good hair day. Whatever puts that extra spring in your step is the way you should go.

Again, the kids are watching, noticing, and will likely emulate—eventually. For example, if they see that you are booking manicures, they will prioritize these for themselves too. Nails were always a big thing in our house, mainly because I'm a reformed nail biter. Manicures were my way to quit this habit. My girls witnessed my regular visits over the years, skipped the nail-biting stage, and went straight to the request for manicures. I thought, why not? Until this day, the girls take pride in their nails and book their own appointments for a little *me time*.

Let me ask YOU, what puts that extra spring into your step? Please say it out loud. Whatever you just declared as "your thing", please time manage 20 minutes or more to do it later today, and every day you feel you need it.

Remove Yourself from the Present, Just for a Moment

Sometimes the only thing that would put an extra spring in my step, especially when particularly stressed or when I had writer's block, was a brisk walk or a dance around the room. Yes, a dance around the room to a fabulous vocal that would pick me up. It's the same PR concept we discussed in Chapter 3 when prepping for public speaking to get rid of the *shpilkes* (nervous energy in Yiddish). Shake it out, baby!

Rather than beat myself up about this or that, start sweating over a looming deadline, or freak out about some situation, like when I have no idea what next to put on a page, I remove (present tense—I still do this) myself from my surroundings and time manage some spontaneous exercise, dancing, or stretching into my day, even if for a few minutes. I breathe deeply a lot too.

Simply giving myself a short mental break from having to produce something brilliant right then and there, and with some physical activity, helps to clear my head and get the ideas flowing again.

Walks are a particularly great opportunity to also get some fresh air, stretch your muscles, and be nice to yourself. You can also take your music with you and dance throughout your walk. Yes, I've done this too. I simply smile at onlookers wondering what's gotten into me. They smile back or ignore. All good.

It's all about being nice to yourself because mommy counts too. What a concept!!

When you have finished with this chapter, I encourage you to take a walk or throw a spontaneous dance party for yourself. Clear your mind. Think of something other than work and only about what makes you happy.

Or think about nothing at all—which is the ultimate mind sorbet.

Listen to nature. People watch. Count how many red cars go by. Whatever. Just relax your brain and move your body.

My yoga teacher friend always says: Movement is medicine. My physical therapist sister always reminds me that if it's physical, it's therapy. And I have another wonderful friend who insists that motion is lotion.

No matter how you phrase it, all three are absolutely right: the more you move, the better you will feel, and the more productive you'll be later.

You see, my friend, self-care doesn't have to cost money. In fact, my very favorite form of self-care is standing with my arms stretched to my sides, wrapped in a lovely breeze, compliments of nature. It's an added bonus to any outdoor activity.

I do this at home during my walks if the opportunity presents. I've also done this during client visits if I've found myself outside, like when I was the press rep at an agritech company that had groves and groves of fruit trees.

I invite you to do the same the next time you feel a breeze. Stretch your arms to the side, close your eyes, and enjoy. It offers a few moments of serenity that can lift your spirits and breathe new energy into your day, your very, very, BUSY day of unending deadlines.

Remember:

- Help your kids prioritize by defining goals, then setting strategies and tactics
- Teach them that there is self-fulfillment in doing good work on time

- Teach them that meeting deadlines is an important function of a family dynamic
- Prioritize your own self-care!

If you would like to practice applying the public relations strategies above to your own story, please use your cell phone camera to scan the QR code below or use the hyperlink to access the free workbook that will walk you through the process.

https://prfor.life/the-power-of-pr-parenting-login-page-qr/

CHAPTER 10

BEING PART OF THE SOLUTION

In this chapter:
- Knowing your value and potential
- Separating perception from reality with respect to diversity, inclusion, and acceptance
- Focusing on exposure and education
- Finding the same same and the different different

My first job out of college was at a small, non-union NBC TV affiliate station in a small Ohio town. Working at a non-union station meant more hands-on experience. As a weekend anchor and weekday reporter, I wrote my own copy, interviewed newsmakers, and edited my own video and reporter packages, like those 1 to 2-minute field stories you see on the news.

I was no stranger to small-town living. I grew up in a suburb of Harrisburg, the capital of Pennsylvania. We lived in a neighborhood on top of one mountain facing another.

I was 21 when I first drove to Ohio, in July 1986, in the car my parents temporarily lent me. I was thrilled to have landed a coveted on-air job, literally two weeks after graduating with a BS in Broadcast Journalism from Boston University. I was lucky to be starting my career so quickly, and I knew it. I had hoped to learn as much as I could and was excited about the journey in front of me and the people I would meet along the way.

One evening, I had just finished producing and anchoring the 11 p.m. weekend news. It was cold outside. I was tired. It had been a very long day. I walked the two minutes to my car parked in the lot in front of the studio, a nondescript office building with an American flag waving proudly outside on a tall flagpole.

I unlocked the door on the driver's side, slipped onto the freezing seat in front of the frigid steering wheel, turned on the ignition, put the automatic car in reverse, and pressed down on the gas pedal. Though the wheels spun furiously, the car stood still.

I raised my foot and tried again. No progress.

I looked at the porch lights of the television studio in front of me that lit up the dark night. I didn't understand. Why was the car not moving?

Frustrated and confused, I got out of the car and went to have a look, first from the side and then from behind. It was pitch black in the parking lot and very hard to see. Mind you, this was before smartphones, and I didn't have a spare flashlight on me. It took a minute or two for my eyes to adjust to the night.

Then I spotted the problem.

Someone had placed a heavy brick behind both of my rear tires.

I let out a big sigh. I thought: *Who? Why? Should I be scared?*

I looked again toward the front of the station building, then around the dark parking lot. There was no one there, at least not that I could see. I guessed I was alone.

I moved the bricks from behind my wheels and placed them in front of my car on the grass that separated the station building from the parking lot, so they wouldn't disturb anyone else. I returned to my car and drove home with the message received: I wasn't wanted there.

Knowing Your Value and Potential, While Paying Your Dues

I woke up the next morning and called my mentor, the former managing editor at the TV station I had done a summer internship at between my junior and senior years in college. I first introduced you to him at the beginning of this book in Chapter 2 when we talked about copywriting.

I told him what had happened and asked if I had stayed long enough to move on from a professional point of view.

"Marjie, you have to give it at least six months, kid. Sorry," he said in his radio-host-like deep voice.

I didn't like what I heard, but I understood that this was what had to be done if I wanted to continue in the industry.

I put my big girl pants on, dug my stiletto heels in, took a deep breath—actually, lots of deep breaths—grew a thicker skin, kept my eye on the donut, and prepared for a stormy rest of my time in Ohio.

That was the bad news. The good news: Around this time the ratings came out, and the numbers for my time on the air were way up. Even if certain members of the staff at the station didn't want me there, enough of the viewing audience did. Some, not wanting me to succeed, were furious.

What exactly did my colleagues have against me? Was it because I was different somehow? Maybe because I was considered from the big city, having recently moved from Boston, and they didn't like city folk in this part of the country? Maybe because I am Jewish, and the town, at least then, had a very small number of Jewish families? (In fact, at the station, there were only three Jews: one on-air talent (me), one female technician, and the general manager.) Or maybe they just didn't like me, for whatever their reasons. Hey, not everyone likes everyone.

I knew for certain the weather anchor wanted me out. The news director had picked me over her for the weekday reporter/weekend anchor opening. She was livid and told me straight to my face that she would do anything to get rid of me and take my job. At every chance, she undercut me and spewed negativity in my direction. But did she hate me enough to cause damage to my car or potentially put me in danger?

I never did find out who placed those bricks behind my car or why. One of the camera people I asked about it chalked it up to a practical joke. I let it go and didn't make a big deal of it. I did, however, learn early in my career to keep my eyes wide open.

My mentor had said six months—so six months it would be before I would start applying for a job elsewhere and eventually land a position in Boston, one of the top markets in the country, as an associate producer of special projects. In that role, I was part of the production team that won a New England Emmy award.

Those six months in Ohio, though, were my introduction to the concept of *paying your dues*. So, I did my best to ignore the weather anchor and fit in, even adopting local phrases into my repertoire. One that remains a favorite until today: "He doesn't know his elbow [or ass, depending on your company] from apple butter."

Though I did make a few lovely friends during this time, truth be told, I don't think the Jewish girl from Boston ever really fit in there. And, when I left, the weather anchor proudly assumed the job I had vacated. I thought: *Really? They rewarded her? Whatever. I'm out of here.*

Enjoy the Commonalities and Celebrate the Differences

Developing a thicker skin during those early days actually helped me weather other nasty challenges and vicious people throughout my career as I continued to pay my dues. It also helped me deal with antisemitism and anti-Israel sentiment, like when I went to buy some cold medicine during a PR assignment in Europe, and the initially friendly pharmacist turned ice cold when he learned that I was visiting from Israel.

In my opinion, hate and fear are not emotions we are born with but rather are learned from a bad experience or from negative teachings. Just like hate and fear can be learned, they can also be unlearned with a positive experience or positive teachings. I had this exact experience when I first started working at the Israeli Consulate.

Important: This is not a political discussion but a human-nature discussion. So please read on with this in mind.

When I began my job as the media liaison, Israel didn't have diplomatic relations with any of its Arab neighbors, except for Egypt. Then came the Oslo Accords in 1993, and in what felt like overnight, evening cocktail parties with previously defined foes became the norm. Once considered enemies, I was now dining and sipping wine with what seemed like nice people. It was time to let go of the preconceptions I had been taught and to open my mind. And on the flip side, it was my honor to be part of the delegation representing Israel, hopefully inspiring our counterparts to do the same.

I also embraced this opportunity to meet and socialize with new friends, the most wonderful byproduct of successful diplomacy.

One of my new friends was from Lebanon. We hung out regularly, and they even invited me to attend an evening meal at the home of their family. We arrived about an hour before the meal was served, and my friend noticed that their mother needed help folding the laundry, which included bed linen.

My friend held up the mattress sheet and commented with a friendly but instructional tone, "Everyone just rolls these into a ball and shoves them into the closet, but there IS an actual way to fold them."

My friend then proceeded to teach me how to fold a mattress sheet. I thought: *Wow, folding laundry. It doesn't get much more universal than this. Everyone does the wash, dries it, and folds it, or at least tries to.* Until today, I think of this moment every time I'm folding sheets.

With the laundry folded, it was then time for dinner. My friend's family was quite lovely. They knew I was Jewish and worked for the Israeli government, and I was still welcomed warmly and treated with respect. They even introduced me to some new foods. It was an enjoyable and educational evening that made an impact on my thinking.

During the early Oslo days, my understanding was reinforced that there are good and bad people in every community. There are those who just want to live their lives and do the best they can for their children. And there are those whose sole purpose is destruction and fist-clenching power for themselves. Just like every family has that crazy uncle or cousin—so too does every community have its good and rotten apples.

Let's talk about some of the good apples, the ones who want to make our world a more tolerant and better place.

Years later, I was on a PR assignment accompanying a client to the World Economic Forum in Tianjin, China. You've heard me talk about this trip in an earlier chapter. The World Economic Forum was, to put it simply, a spectacular experience. It was attended by people from all over the world and from all backgrounds. Everyone was different, and everyone was the same. There was no room for prejudice, only for discussions on how to move the world forward and to work together in harmony to do so. At least, that's what I witnessed, and I loved every second.

Following the Forum in Tianjin, I had an opportunity to visit Beijing for an overnight, to tour a little and have dinner with a Chinese friend.

I first met my Chinese friend when she was working in Israel. During her time in Israel, we became close enough friends that she would hang out with my family on occasion. In fact, one evening, she cooked us an authentic Chinese dinner with Isaac as her sous-chef. My kids adored her and loved learning about China and sampling the authentic Chinese cuisine.

We kept in touch for a few years after she returned to China, which is how we were able to connect for dinner during my visit to attend the World Economic Forum. She was charming as always, and my family was anxious to know how she was doing when I arrived home.

Though we lived hours away by plane and came from different cultures, our similarities were many, like love of family and a desire to do well professionally. And our differences, well, we celebrated those, especially during meals.

Did you know that for dinner, the Chinese eat their cold dishes first, followed by their hot dishes? This means that dessert might come first! Also, at breakfast, the Chinese serve noodles, rice, buns, and meat, very similar to a Western dinner.

The more you open your mind to other cultures, the more you will discover and the more fun you will have. A big lesson for us as parents and for our kids.

Teaching Open-mindedness Through Exposure and Education

As a PR representative, I have always been courteous and polite to everyone, no matter what, in person and on the phone. Aside from being part of the job, it's also how I try to operate when I'm off the clock. And most times, though I might pick up on an accent during a call, I have no idea what the people I am speaking with look like, what their religion is, or where their family originates. This includes the many journalists, investors, clients, and family members of patients looking for clinical trial information that I've spoken with over the decades. (My specialty is medical public relations, and many of my clients are sponsoring clinical studies at any given time.)

Now, if I may be frank, I don't really care about the origins, religion, or appearances of the people I speak with on the phone. As far as I'm concerned, we are all God's children. To borrow a phrase from one of my brothers-in-law: What's important when assessing people, and especially when choosing company, is to *look for the golden heart.*

Is this person kind? Well-meaning? Are they speaking to you respectfully? If so, the rest is gravy, and a potentially wonderful gravy at that.

Assuming peaceful interaction, differences are pluses rather than something to fear or hate, and we should encourage our kids to be inclusive rather than divisive.

I don't mean to be preachy about this, but it is something that I feel strongly about and wanted to teach my kids, not only in words but also in deeds.

I tried to teach them how to love, not hate, to celebrate rather than to fear differences, and to be comfortable enough with themselves to even be able to smooth the way for someone else who might contrast with the rest.

I saw for myself how hatred and fear are learned. And if it's learned, someone is doing the teaching. I say to all those teachers out there, and to you as a parent—ditch the negativity, and in its place, let's teach love, respect, and acceptance. It takes much less energy to be kind and brings on a much better feeling and outcome.

You ask: How?

As a career public relations professional, emphasis on *relations,* I've found it takes a three-pronged approach: a strong sense of **self**, complemented with **exposure** and **education**.

Let's start with a strong sense of self. First, you need to be comfortable in your own skin. When you know who you are, appreciate yourself (at least most of the time) and are confident in what you can bring to the table in terms of any given skill set, then you can contribute positively in some way to any situation.

We've spent chapters in this book talking about how to use international PR methods to raise confident kids with a strong sense of self. We've talked about honing self-reliance, performance and presentation skills as well as teaching our kids how to behave with grace during successes and failures. All of these experiences lead to a strong sense of self that can be used towards producing goodness and maybe even an extraordinary outcome.

Now let's fast track to exposure and education.

One way we exposed our kids and educated them to the outside world was by hosting a revolving door of visitors from abroad whom we had met through work, like my Chinese friend.

My kids have also met my American high school and university friends from various religions and backgrounds. Some of these friends and their children flew to Israel to celebrate one or more of our Bar and Bat Mitzvahs. And we went to visit them in the U.S. Their kids are my kids, and my kids are their kids. All in the family.

Everyone was invited and welcomed, on both sides of the ocean. This policy helped my children gain a wider view of the world and the different types of people who live in it.

I'd like to ask you—who from your present or past could show your children another way to cook, a new song to sing, a new approach to problem solving? Invite them to visit for an afternoon or even a weekend if you have the bandwidth.

In the early years, when we'd live in the U.S. during the summers, Guy attended day camp and Noa Lee attended a kindergarten class where both the staff and the kids came from different backgrounds and communities. In fact, it was at this kindergarten where Noa Lee finally started speaking fluent English. Until then, she understood but would speak mostly *Henglish*, a mixture of Hebrew and English.

You don't need a passport to broaden the viewpoint of your children. Where nearby your house could you send your kids to safely learn about a different culture or religion? It could come in the form of an art class or perhaps a sports event like football, soccer, gymnastics or skiing. Athletes come from all over the world to compete. Maybe there's a competition close by that you can attend. Or maybe one of the kids at school is celebrating a religious rite of passage, and your child has been invited to the ceremony and the party that follows. Same same, different different. What a grand opportunity.

Chances to teach love rather than hate arise regularly, sometimes when you least expect them. Often, they are born out of an innocent observation. I remember the first time my children noticed and asked me why people have different skin colors. The opportunity to teach love was smack in front of me.

"Sweeties, everyone has a different shade of skin color. All are beautiful," I answered.

They nodded their heads and from that point on, for my kids, skin color was, well, just that, skin color. Of course, they learned about the specific histories of different peoples and communities, but skin color was irrelevant to their showing respect or developing friendships.

As they got older, the passport helped. I can't deny it. My kids were invited to participate in school exchange programs and summer adventures abroad. This is when they had an opportunity to travel and live with kids from different countries and cultures, and with different religious beliefs.

Guy backpacked in Alaska for three weeks with a group of kids from around the world including a lovely French Catholic young lady and a charming Muslim young man from Jordan, who nicknamed Guy, "Cousin". The *cousins* helped each other climb a very tall, slippery glacier. Talk about trust.

Noa Lee was part of an exchange program with a junior high school in Germany. She lived with a Christian, German family who had a daughter Noa Lee's age, and this same girl stayed with us for a week or so during the Passover holiday. This young lady was very shy, so I tried to notice what she was willing to eat and bought a bunch of it, which made her smile and even exclaim "Oh, yum!" I think it was a version of sliced turkey. Again, food is always a good icebreaker!

One year, Maya attended an area school with a diverse student population, which instantly accepted her and, even today, the friends she made there remain some of her best. Okay, not exactly an adventure to a far-off land, but some of the net results were the same.

Although there's no place like home, there's also no substitute for exploration and seeing life through the eyes of someone else. Everyone does it differently. Not better or worse necessarily, just differently.

Respect. Kindness. Tolerance. Patience.

We must teach our kids early to be part of the solution rather than the problem and to approach situations in such a way to prevent problems from arising in the first place. This is the best way to combat prejudice in the long term.

Now let's get into the practicality of it.

If there's a new kid at school, even if they seem a bit odd, remind your child that this new kid may be having a tough time transitioning to a new place, has real feelings and an interest in making friends. My days at the small station in Ohio, though a fantastic professional experience where I learned a lot, were tough socially. Try to make it an easier experience for that new kid in school and for their parents too who are also trying to adjust to a new environment.

When you or your child meets someone who comes from a place that you've only read about but have never visited or from a background you've only heard things about but have never experienced yourself, give this child and their parents the benefit of the doubt and the chance to show the kind of people they are before passing judgment. Try not to be like the pharmacist in Europe who assumed I was bad because I was from Israel. Rather follow the advice of my brother-in-law: look for the golden heart. Also, stand up for what is right and help when possible.

A brighter tomorrow begins with teaching our kids that the world has all types of people in it, not only ones who look or believe the way we do. As parents, it's up to us to use diplomacy and public relations practices to teach our kids to find common ground and make lasting friendships.

Yes, we should have pride in who we are and the values that we bring to the table, but the faster we learn to respect the other guy and adopt an inclusive attitude, the smoother the future will be. The menu will be more interesting too!

Remember:

- Trust in yourself and your abilities, even when under fire
- Turn negatives into positives and teach your kids to have an open mind
- Appreciate likenesses and celebrate differences
- Teach your kids early to be part of the solution to prejudice by relying on four principles above all: respect, tolerance, kindness, and patience

If you would like to practice applying the public relations strategies above to your own story, please use your cell phone camera to scan the QR code below or use the hyperlink to access the free workbook that will walk you through the process.

https://prfor.life/the-power-of-pr-parenting-login-page-qr/

POSTSCRIPT

Being a parent is the best job and the hardest job. Though every kid is different, and none come with instructions, the unconditional love that transpires between you and your child is priceless. If for no other reason than to respect this unconditional love, we have to do our very best for our kids from the moment they arrive until the day we take our last breath, no matter how much they test us from time to time.

A good part of parenting is taking our best guess, based on our talents, skills and experiences, many of which we learn from our professions. We also compare notes with other parents along the way and try out what has worked for them and try to avoid what didn't. I am guessing you picked up this book as another way to do this.

I am just like you, a working mom trying to make my best go at it. One difference, perhaps: You may still have babies, little kids or early teens, whereas I'm at halftime. My kids are now young adults.

As I was looking back at the last 25 years and simultaneously taking a good look at my children today, it surprised me to understand how heavily I had relied on public relations practices when parenting. Remember, it wasn't intentional while I was doing it, so the realization truly blew my mind.

Hindsight is 20/20, and I wanted you to benefit, by sitting with you over a cup of coffee and sharing what I could to make your life at least a little easier. I genuinely hope the PR practices that have worked for me will work for you too, when you are parenting, and for your life in general.

Throughout this book, I invited you into my personal and professional world, shared behind the scenes glimpses, and confided in you some of my most private thoughts. (You can keep a secret right?)

When you close the back cover of this book or slide your e-reader version to the very last page, I would like to invite you to pause for a moment or two or three. Please close your eyes for a couple of minutes or stare off in the distance if you prefer—and reflect.

What PR practices did you learn from this book that could help you through the next minute, hour, day, week, month or even the coming years?

Remember to look at time in a way that works for you. You don't ONLY have 15 minutes; you have 15 WHOLE minutes.

Maybe you are in the middle of a crisis. Deep breath and do your best to compartmentalize, problem solve and act, NOT react, for no other reason than because you have to. And I know you can. Talk yourself through it if necessary.

Perhaps you are navigating a challenging or thrilling situation with all eyes on you. In the spotlight or not, I encourage you to set an example for your children and show them how to do it with grace, even if you need to admit you've made a mistake. It's okay to make mistakes. We are all human.

Be aware of your surroundings and of the actions and reactions of your kids and encourage them to communicate with you and vocalize their needs. You can only help if they are willing to invite you into their world and tell you truthfully what's going on. Create the kind of environment that will encourage them to do this.

Prepare your kids for the good and the bad in advance so they will know what to do when a *situation* arises. Teach them how to turn things around when necessary.

On a daily basis, do what you can to instill high self-esteem in your child. This is the main cornerstone of creating a strong and confident adult who can contribute to society and help their fellow person. It's important to make this cornerstone as solid as possible. A hug is a great way to start.

And finally, PLEASE take good care of YOU and be true to yourself. Take pride in who you are, while remembering to celebrate diversity and teach kindness.

I've enjoyed our coffee together and look forward to continuing our conversation in the future.

In the meantime, I am wishing you the absolute very best as you apply your existing or newly learned PR skills to parenting.

One final reminder, if you'd like to practice applying the public relations practices in this book to your own story, click on the QR code below to access the free workbook that will walk you through the process.

Peace, love and light, my friend.

ACKNOWLEDGEMENTS

It takes a village to raise a family. It also takes a village to write and publish a book.

This has been an incredible journey and I am very grateful for the support systems that helped make it happen.

My Family

Sending loads of appreciation and love to my husband Isaac and my children, Guy, Noa Lee and Maya. Kids, you are and always will be my inspiration and the light that fills my world with joy. I love you to the moon and back and couldn't be prouder that you are my legacy. And to my husband, thank you for an amazing partnership. You are my best friend and forever love.

I'd like to also thank my family and friends for their advice, perspective, humor and positive energy. A success for one of us is a success for all of us. I am blessed to have you in my life and I humbly share the achievement of this milestone (the publishing of my first book) with you.

The Book Team

Every author needs a champion to shepherd their project to success. I am no different. Sending loads of love and appreciation to my champions at Muse Literary. Thank you Sara Connell and Patricia Fors for believing in me and my mission, appreciating my work and guiding me on this journey with patience and grace.

I'd also like to send a big shout out to Thought Leader Academy developmental editor Aubyn Keefe for her precise instruction, direct feedback and for making an overwhelming process fun.

I am also sending love and appreciation to (in alphabetical order): Lisa Ansbacher, Dr. Lorry Leigh Belhumeur, Shari Biery, MaryBeth Bisson, Carol Cohen, Lisa Deck, Cindy Garnick, Natalie Tull Greene, Dr. Keren Hadad-Leibovich, Dr. Kathy Hirsh-Pasek, Dr. Dafna Katzir-Goldenboum, Donna Kendrick, Alex Kuisis, Sharon Lewis, Jeff Pasek, Aubrey Sanchez, Julie Schwartz, Daniel Shanken, Mandell Shanken, Mayor Shanken, Dr. Serena Shanken-Skwersky, William Skwersky, Daliah Sklar, Jaymie Velasquez, Wendee Villanueva, Beth Yakoby and Justine Zwerling.

Also, a special thank you to my talented author's headshot team: fashion photographer Dean Avisar, fashion designer HILI ARI, stylist Qamai Harel and makeup and hair artist Refael Baron.

I am blessed to have all of the people noted above in my corner. Again, thanks to all.

YOU

My primary goal in writing this book is to reach and help as many as possible.

So, I would also like to thank YOU for choosing The Power of PR Parenting and for taking the time to read it. I know there are tons of parenting books out there. I very much appreciate your picking this one from the pile.

I hope this book has given you some new and helpful ideas and ways to approach current and future challenges. I am wishing you good health, much success and every happiness.

Marjie Hadad

ENDNOTES

1. Mayo Clinic staff, "Pacifiers: Are they good for your baby?" mayoclinic.org https://www.mayoclinic.org/healthy-lifestyle/infant-and-toddler-health/in-depth/pacifiers/art-20048140#:~:text=A%20pacifier%20might%20help%20reduce%20the%20risk%20of,into%20an%20effective%20nursing%20routine.%20Pacifiers%20are%20disposable.
2. Delta Dental, "Baby pacifiers: Pros and cons," https://www.deltadentalins.com/oral_health/baby_pacifiers.html
3. Delta Dental, "Baby pacifiers: Pros and cons," https://www.deltadentalins.com/oral_health/baby_pacifiers.html
4. Stieg, C. "Raising kids bilingual can make them more attentive and efficient as adults," *CNBC.com*, Jan. 22, 2021, https://www.cnbc.com/2021/01/22/growing-up-bilingual-can-improve-attentiveness-efficiency-study.html
5. D'Souza et al. "Early bilingual experience is associated with change detection ability in adults," *Scientific Reports*, Jan. 22, 2021, https://www.nature.com/articles/s41598-021-81545-5
6. Parents Editors, "How to Teach Your Child a Foreign Language," parents.com, Oct. 3, 2005, https://www.parents.com/baby/development/intellectual/how-to-teach-your-child-a-foreign-language/
7. Miao, X. "At what age do children start losing their baby teeth?" mayoclinic.org, https://www.mayoclinic.org/healthy-lifestyle/childrens-health/expert-answers/baby-teeth/faq-20058532

8. Kapner et al. "The Best and Worst Foods for Your Teeth," US San Diego Health, June 1, 2021, https://myhealth.ucsd.edu/wellness/mentalhealth/1,4062

9. "Dark Chocolate Has Some Benefits for Your Oral Health," Young Family Dental, https://youngfamilydental.com/dark-chocolate-has-some-benefits-for-your-oral-health

10. Richter, F. "COVID-19 has caused a huge amount of lost working hours," World Economic Forum, February 4, 2021, https://www.weforum.org/agenda/2021/02/covid-employment-global-job-loss/

11. "Missing and Exploited Children," Office of Juvenile Justice and Delinquency Prevention, https://ojjdp.ojp.gov/programs/missing-and-exploited-children#

12. Mrkonjić, E. "20 Heartbreaking Missing Children Statistics [2021 Update]," The High Court, Oct. 12, 2021, https://thehighcourt.co/missing-children-statistics/

13. Weinstein Agrawal, et al. "Sexual crime and harassment on public transportation: A study," Metro, May 14, 2020, https://www.metro-magazine.com/10111994/sexual-crime-and-harassment-on-public-transportation-a-study

14. Weinstein Agrawal, et al. "Sexual crime and harassment on public transportation: A study," Metro, May 14, 2020, https://www.metro-magazine.com/10111994/sexual-crime-and-harassment-on-public-transportation-a-study

15. Numbeo, "Cost of Living in Israel," https://www.numbeo.com/cost-of-living/country_result.jsp?country=Israel#:~:text=A%20single%20person%20estimated%20monthly%20costs%20are%201%2C068.33%24,on%20average%2C%2032.76%25%20lower%20than%20in%20United%20States.

ABOUT THE AUTHOR

Marjie Hadad is an international public relations expert, the general manager of Must Have Communication & Consulting, an author, an award-winning TV producer, as well as a coach and a speaker on how to apply public relations strategies to parenting, life and careers. *The Power of PR Parenting* is her first book. Marjie holds a BS in Broadcast Journalism and an MA in International Relations both from Boston University. She is married and is the mother of three children. She lives in Israel and the United States. For more information: www.mhc-pr.com and PRFor.Life

> If you liked this book and it provided you with some value, I'd be happy if you could post a review. Thank you in advance for sharing your feedback.

Printed in the USA
CPSIA information can be obtained
at www.ICGtesting.com
LVHW041925161023
761253LV00004B/426